Cornwall
The People and Culture of an Industrial Camelot 1890-1980

CARL OBLINGER

Commonwealth of Pennsylvania
PENNSYLVANIA HISTORICAL
AND MUSEUM COMMISSION
Harrisburg, 1984

ISBN 0-89271-028-4

Copyright ©1984 Commonwealth of Pennsylvania

Cover picture: New underground miners at No. 3 mine entrance, Cornwall Ore Bank Company, on opening day 1921. All photographs were contributed by individual miners interviewed and by retired Bethlehem Steel Company photographer R. Jay Angelo, unless otherwise credited.

SUPPORTED BY A GRANT FROM:

**PENNSYLVANIA
HUMANITIES
COUNCIL**

A STATEWIDE FUNDING ORGANIZATION FUNDED IN PART BY THE NATIONAL ENDOWMENT FOR THE HUMANITIES

Opinions and ideas expressed in this book do not necessarily represent the views of the Pennsylvania Humanities Council or those of the National Endowment for the Humanities.

Preface

THE history that will be found in this book may be unlike any that the reader may previously have read. It is not an academic study strictly, for the academic approach to local history, whether it be written in the guise of ethnic, political, oral or some form of social history, is not satisfactory. Academic history focuses on the concerns of specialists and, therefore, means very little to members of the larger society. It does not adequately convey the real-life experiences of people who have lived in a particular place; and it asks for a specialized knowledge that the general audience does not have.

What we have produced, therefore, is a participatory history—a history that attempts to answer questions raised by people who have patiently offered us their knowledge, experiences and, in a sense, their souls. The purpose of this is to know what life in Cornwall has been, and how conditions in the community came to be as they now are.

This simple requirement pushed me beyond the mechanics of doing just another oral history project. I had to escape the confines of my classroom training as a historian and develop a new, more encompassing view of oral history. No longer could questions be directed only to my particular interests and concerns. Instead, I had to imagine what it might mean to remain for a lifetime, by choice or necessity, in Cornwall; to raise children there with the hope that they would find ways of staying in the community; and to labor daily in jobs which *appeared* to offer little psychic satisfaction. This was a difficult task for me, but one that had to be accomplished.

There are dangers, however, in taking a view totally from inside Cornwall and presenting it as the complete story. After all, the recollections presented here are the stories of long-time employees who regarded as benign their relationship with their employer. I had, after all, only limited access to disgruntled employees. Furthermore, the investigation of the Cornwall workers' world was complicated by the local legend which portrayed the previous owners, the Colemans and the Freemans, as benevolent and paternalistic. In its simplest form, this legend depicts a late nineteenth-century and early twentieth-century community of workers and employers which was harmonious and cooperative.

The closing of the mines and the rude awakening to a realization that the present company was not a benevolent provider is also what this book is about. The unanswered questions, the unfulfilled promises, and the disillusionment left miners "confused." It is this "confusion" upon which I hope to shed some light.

It was Camelot here. It only rained at night.—Former Cornwall laborer, 1976.

Acknowledgments

L EBANON County and the Cornwall area are especially sensitive to
  networks of friends and family. I relied on those networks to gain
entree to the Cornwall community for my interviews. My friend and col-
league, Mike Kristovensky, Director of the Lebanon Office of Aging,
provided the crucial introduction to Mike Stefonich of Cornwall, who in
turn introduced me to other community people. One of those community
people to whom I was introduced was Albert Perini, who immediately
called everybody he knew in the borough, fed me delicious ham sandwiches, kept my glass full of Coke, and warmed my ear constantly with
humorous stories of the mines. His and Mike Stefonich's homes served
as the home bases for my forays into the surrounding community.

I especially enjoyed the public discussion and slide show a panel of
miners and I conducted on the Cornwall community, 1880-1972, in the
Sacred Heart Parish Center, Cornwall, November 16, 1981. In preparation for that night, in which 250 community people crammed into the
Parish Center, I received support from Father Stephen F. Jordan, the
pastor, Hy White of Radio Station WLBR, Charles Neil and Mike
Kristovensky. The publication of this book should be the occasion for
another such community event.

The Pennsylvania Historical and Museum Commission was supportive
of this project. The work was carried out under Harry E. Whipkey,
Director of the Bureau of Archives and History and John B. B. Trussell,
Jr., Chief, Division of History. The work was begun under John E. Bod-
nar, former chief, now at Indiana University, Bloomington. Harold L.
Myers, Associate Historian, looked after its publication. Lillian Ulrich,
Terry Musgrave and Linda Ries helped with the photographs. Matthew
S. Magda supported my efforts throughout every phase of transcription,
editing and publication. We had many discussions concerning the meaning of our findings and the future direction of our work. The project
benefited from the transcript-typing of Pat McKee and Joanne Born-
man. Renée Lux of Cornwall Iron Furnace provided very timely assistance in typing the final manuscript. John Robinson, Ms. Lux's supervisor at the Pennsylvania Historical and Museum Commission-adminis-
tered historic site, took the initiative in "loaning" Renée to us. I also appreciate the opportunity John gave me to speak to the Cornwall Iron
Furnace Associates and to "relax" in his inner sanctum. Mary Brod, a
former member of the Cornwall Furnace staff, and Paul Doutrich of the
Bureau for Historic Preservation each offered timely and pointed criti-
cisms of the introduction on two different occasions.

Finally, my daughter Jennifer, son Erik, stepdaughter Chris Gabel, and stepson Jim Gabel all offered criticism and perspectives different from mine. My wife Margery supported me during this endeavor and added her voice to the children's. I think this work will not be quite "so boring" because of their efforts.

I conducted all the interviews in this book, which were supported by a generous Pennsylvania Humanities Council grant, in 1981 and 1982. The only exceptions are the Rita Steffensen and Hilda Perini interviews, which Ellen Wyle of the Hershey Museum of American History conducted in August, 1981. In a sense the people of Cornwall are the co-authors of this book. They opened their homes, their store of memories, and their hearts to someone who appreciates their history and who also gained twenty pounds.

CARL OBLINGER

Interviewees:

Robert Arnold, Sr.
Mrs. Marian Davis
Mrs. Warner Franklin
Matthew "Tip" Karinch
Earl Kohr
Russell "Red" McDaniels
Charles Neil
Albert Perini
Hilda Stahley Perini
Peter Rossini, Jr.
Mike Stefonich
Mrs. P. L. Steffensen
John Joseph Yocklovich
Lester Yorty

Introduction

T O MANY people in the Lebanon Valley of Pennsylvania, the Cornwall Ore Mines typify the whole range of America's experience with industrialization. Local retired iron-ore miners love to take visitors to the mile-long open pit that is positioned between Miner's Village and Burd-Coleman. There they point out various levels within this pit and recall the two and a quarter centuries that the pit has been in operation. To these retired miners, who spent more than three-fourths of their years in the underground mines and the open pit, this hole in the ground is a constant reminder of the all-encompassing industrial and social worlds in which they and their predecessors once lived.

Resonant in the recollections are the values and behavior of workers immersed in the amazing paternalistic world of a twentieth-century industrial giant and dependent upon it for their entire existence. Their diverse backgrounds in the long run mattered little, be they "Dutch" from the farms and villages of Lebanon County, sons and daughters of immigrants, or blacks from the homesteads of the South. Bethlehem Steel housed most workers' families, fed them in times of extreme depression, found them jobs when none was available in the open pit or underground mines, educated their children in the borough schools, and governed them at the borough level. At their own initiative the workers developed strong networks of family and village loyalties, reveled in sporting activi-

The open-pit mine at Cornwall. The flood of 1925, shown here, filled it and the underground mines with water.

1

ties and recreation, principally attended two churches, and drank and sang together. Their own activities and cultural inclination, in fact, reinforced the conservative and paternalistic bent of Bethlehem Steel.

In this small book the memories of Cornwall's people are presented. The bulk of the memoirs span the entire twentieth century, from the time the Cornwall Ore Bank Company still reflected the influence of the original owners, the Colemans, to the closing of the mines in 1973. A particularly crucial period to all, though, was the period in which the workers lost their jobs in the mines (1932-1936) and the period in which the local of the United Steelworkers struggled to establish and maintain its existence (1937-1942). The oral histories are especially compelling which detail the initial movement of the ethnic and black workers into the area, and their struggles to establish an emotionally adequate and sanitary life in the small villages. These pages also depict individuals who established substantial careers in the technical and union worlds. But mostly they relate the struggle of workers to come to grips with industrialization and with a company which enclosed them in a paternalistic world.

This book finds its theme in my effort to ground the history of Cornwall and its miners in a more precise history of capitalism in America. The vignettes presented track the socially complex transition from the industrial capitalism of the Cornwall Ore Bank Company to the monopoly capitalism of Bethlehem Steel, suggesting how the miners and their wives understood, engaged in and responded to changes in production, safety and relationships with bosses and the company. In Cornwall the story is interesting because the people had to cope with the legacy of paternalism from the Cornwall Ore Bank Company. Though the larger economic changes transforming industrial landscapes and relationships in America did not initially intrude on Cornwall, by the late 1930s and the 1940s change was apparent. The whole question after that was how long the old mines and old ways could resist the onslaught of a changing world order.

I

Ironmaster Peter Grubb began this industrial plantation in the 1730s. In 1734 he paid £135 for three hundred acres in what was then Lancaster County. Three years later, Grubb bought 142.5 additional acres, including three hills of magnetite ore "rich and abundant, forty feet deep, commencing two feet under the earth's surface." Finally, in 1742, the cautious ironmaster built his first furnace and named it Cornwall after his father's home county in England.

Labor was attracted to the new furnace and adjoining ore diggings by the promise of adequate wages and decent living conditions. Initially, workers lived in log cabins. Later the company built workers small houses of locally quarried limestone. The homes were impressive for

2

their day. Each had two stories, whitewashed walls and sanded floors. The company placed in each home a great iron cauldron for boiling laundry; cooking utensils including plates, spoons, and bowls; pitchers made of local pewter; and forks and knives made of local iron.

Work was primitive and hard at the furnace and in the pit. Men and boys picked and shoveled ore and limestone from the outcroppings on the hills. Then mule-driven, two-wheeled carts hauled the "mine" (ore and limestone) from the pit to the furnaces. Average annual compensation for a laborer in the early nineteenth century was between $180 and $250. Though such a wage seemed adequate, it was not enough to insure savings by the time company clerks deducted rent and the purchase of essential supplies like meat, flour, shoes, soaps, candles, and thread from the company store.

Labor responded in traditional ways to the drudgery and irregular work. It was common for a pit laborer to lose, on the average, six work days a month due to "intoxesitation [sic] with liquor." Time records also indicate that the owners dealt with the problem of "night revelry" by crediting the laborers only half-time for late arrival at work. Part of the problem was the easy availability of whiskey; the ironmaster credited most of the purchases of whiskey on account.

This lack of capital put labor at the mercy of Cornwall's owners from the beginning. Basically powerless (the original labor force comprised Irish and German servants and black slaves), Cornwall's workers had to accommodate themselves to the demands of the owners. Consequently, most relationships at the pit and furnaces had become frozen into formal and elaborate rituals of submission by the late 1700s.

There were reasons other than lack of money which tied the workers to the owners. One of the most important was the absolute splendor with which the principal owners dazzled the workers. Robert Coleman, who inherited Cornwall from the Grubbs in 1798, was among America's first millionaires. In the mid-1800s his heirs built a mansion consisting of fifty-two rooms. It resembled to some an elegantly cluttered museum. Several rooms contained furniture from Napoleon's palace while others were decorated with relics from Pompeii. Besides the mansion, there were a number of other impressive buildings on the Coleman estate. The stable, for example, was a large brownstone structure fitted with stained-glass windows at either end. There were stalls for nineteen horses, while the upper level held quarters for the same number of grooms.

The wealth and dominance of the Coleman family once established were maintained throughout the nineteenth century, and were strengthened by an extraordinary paternalism. The Colemans erected near Cornwall additional housing for the workers, all frame houses painted the same dark red. They paid doctor bills for their employees. And they built

3

schools and a church for the ironworkers' children in Cornwall and hired the best teachers.

Christmas in the Colemans' employ in the mid-nineteenth century was an elaborate affair by any standard. For Christmas dinner the Colemans sent each of the nearly five hundred Cornwall workers a large turkey. All the workers and their families would visit the palatial Coleman mansion in groups at appointed hours. Under the thirty-foot tree were presents of toys for the employees' children. By celebrating Christmas and by establishing other important traditions, the Colemans endeared themselves to every one of their employee families. In return, the workers revered the Colemans, worked hard, and made the Cornwall venture very profitable.

Even as late as the 1930s—long after the holdings were sold to Bethlehem Steel—older workers continued to defer to the Colemans. After some Cornwall laborers were fired upon by a Coleman hunting party, not one dared object to the danger in which they were placed. As one laborer reminisced: "It never entered our heads to complain about their endangering our lives. We were *peasants*. They were nobles!"

II

The wealth of the Colemans depended on their ability to anticipate changes in the market and in the technology of iron-ore production. In the 1840s, the Cornwall operation quietly expanded production, doubling and then tripling its 1832 output. The immediate stimulus to expansion was the tremendous nation-wide demand for iron to build bridges and railroads. The anthracite-coal deposit at Pine Grove, twenty-five miles to the north, could now be mined profitably and shipped to Cornwall to fire the new anthracite furnaces at North Lebanon, Burd-Coleman and North Cornwall. By 1864, the operation produced one hundred thousand tons of pig iron a year, ten times the amount produced for a single year in the 1840s.

The increased capacity of the furnaces caused changes in the techniques of open-pit mining. An elaborate system of terraced mining and blasting—which consisted of working the ore in steps sixteen to twenty feet deep—replaced the random digging in holes dug in the ore beds. The men now worked in organized teams and by the 1860s were hauling their wheelbarrows to openbed railroad cars pulled out of the pits by small engines known as "dinkies." In 1883, two-man drills and dynamite blasting replaced pick and shovel. Because of the depletion of high-grade iron ore by the 1880s, engineers constructed roasting ovens a short distance from the pit to concentrate the lower-grade ore.

Paralleling the changing technology of mining and haulage was the consolidation in 1864 of Cornwall's ninety-six part owners—heirs of Peter Grubb and Robert Coleman—into the Cornwall Ore Bank Com-

Two-man air drills bored as far as eighteen feet; open pit 1915.

pany. Control of all mining was handled by the Cornwall Ore Bank Company, which in turn answered to the joint owners at stockholders' meetings.

In the 1880s, some of the Cornwall Ore Bank Company's holdings passed into the hands of the Pennsylvania Steel Company so the latter could obtain ore for its new Steelton plant. Interested in increasing its output of refined iron ore, the Pennsylvania Steel Company erected a concentrator plant at the site of the Northern Lebanon furnace. This concentrator enabled Pennsylvania Steel to use a lower-grade ore and, eventually, to bring steam shovels into their section of the open pit.

The tremendous increase in production in the period of the 1860s, 1870s and 1880s drew a new breed of worker to Cornwall. Tough, boisterous, hard-working, and hard-drinking, the miners of the late nineteenth century were Cornish and Pennsylvania Dutch. In the early twentieth century the work force expanded to include Mexicans, southern-born blacks, Hungarians, Slovaks and Italians. Except for the blacks and Mexicans, the ethnic miners and their offspring intermarried with the older Dutch population and each other; such intermarriage demonstrated the closeness and dependence which the local workers had with and upon each other. The small communities in the vicinity of the open pit affectionately came to be known, as a consequence of ethnic intermingling, as Dutchtown, Hunkytown and Goosetown.

Between 1916 and 1921, in an effort to acquire iron-ore deposits of its

5

Mine superintendents, Cornwall 1924, Arthur Peterson on the right.

own, Bethlehem Steel Company acquired the Pennsylvania Steel Company holdings and the entire Cornwall Ore Bank Company's holdings, including housing, in a series of purchases. When geological explorations commenced in 1919, Bethlehem located a second ore body to the east, 150 feet below the surface, and discovered in the new holdings that the magnetite ore carried recoverable amounts of copper, gold, silver, sulphur and cobalt. Consequently, Bethlehem Steel opened two underground mines between 1921 and 1927 to exploit the newly found deposits and deplete the old ones.

Bethlehem Steel scoured the continent for skilled engineers and underground miners who could tap the new lode and deplete the old. A new mine superintendent, Arthur Peterson, was recruited from the Upper Peninsula of Michigan. Peter Rossini, a skilled miner with exceptional knowledge of underground mining from Ironton, Minnesota, was hired to help Peterson sink the shaft of No. 3 mine. Similarly, Bethlehem Steel recruited black laborers and some Mexicans to take over the work in the open pit so other, more skilled laborers could be freed for underground mining. The new underground miners, lured beneath the surface by promise of rapid advancement and better money, had an attitude different from the raw-open-pit men of the nineteenth century: though out-

6

wardly tough, many were resigned to a fate of quick death from a chunk of loose ore or a hurtling ore-haulage car.*

III

The most tumultuous period in Cornwall's history was the 1930s. Underground operations were closed in 1931, and production in the open pit ceased entirely between 1933 and 1936. The period was specially trying to miners and their wives, since most Lebanon Countians "would not accept" relief or charity. Jobs were pitifully scarce, and some left Cornwall's company homes to move in with relatives and to be closer to the Civilian Conservation Corps Camp at Indiantown Gap or the Works Progress Administration jobs in Lebanon City. Others in Cornwall were content with self-survival; they drew on their accumulated savings and grew and canned nearly everything needed from their gardens. Bethlehem Steel eased the pressure by neither forcing rent payments nor evicting families from company homes.

Resumption of production in late 1936 led to the first serious challenge of Bethlehem Steel in Cornwall. The then Committee for Industrial Organization (CIO) attempted to organize all of Bethlehem Steel's Lebanon County employees in early 1937. There were serious accumulated grievances against the company and especially the company union in Cornwall. As one local diarist related: "[The success of the strike] will reflect an improvement locally. I have my doubts concerning the advantage of the company union anyway. It is stuffed down the employee's throat, in a manner of a take it or leave it proposition." At particular issue in Cornwall were the forced overtime, production quotas, and meagre wages which neither Bethlehem Steel nor the management of the company union would address.

In the end the CIO could not sustain the strike in Lebanon County and Cornwall. Pressure on the strikers was tremendous. The full force of local opinion was mobilized against them. The Lebanon *Daily News* daily printed letters supporting strikebreakers' right to cross picket lines and ridiculing the stupidity of the strikers. Townspeople harassed strikers in Lebanon by pushing them off the sidewalks. The Lebanon police beat and gassed many of the strikers. Though the strike lasted almost three weeks, shut operations down at Cornwall, and resulted in a five-dollar day, many in Cornwall felt that "the [union] movement was discredited."

*Before a company safety program was implemented, the probability was great that a miner would be seriously injured in his lifetime. Though reportedly safe in the 1920s, '30s and '40s, the mines were in fact dangerous. The main problem was that the primary method of underground mining—shrinkage and pillar—was hazardous. Between 1923 and 1973, 33 men were killed and 873 were seriously injured. Most fatalities occurred in the 1920-1940 period.

7

The real problem was that there wasn't much support initially for unionization among Cornwall workers. Most believed in Bethlehem Steel's good intentions and had a positive attitude toward their work. The underground workers, in particular, did not picture themselves as simply miners, but as skilled workmen—timbermen, mucker drift-trammer, miner's helper, head miner—who could advance to management. Rather than comment abstractly about "management," retired miners would look back and reminisce about a particular mine foreman, a boss or a superintendent who secured them a job and helped them move ahead in the 1920s and 1930s; there was room, they felt, to recognize personal worth and accomplishment. This faith and the relationships which buttressed it are the main reasons the 1937 strike remains so problematic for most of the men even today; it forced both labor and management to perceive Bethlehem Steel and their relationship to it in a new and unfamiliar way.

Family and community response to unionization in 1937 was negative. Traditional social and religious ideals helped little since they served to buttress the position of the company as arbiter of values. Patriarchal families and authoritative religion stressed hierarchy, authority and *familiarity*. Dominant values included steady work and familial well-being; the prominence of the priest, the manager of the mines, and the head of household reinforced the position of the company in local life, and the position of the union *outside* the realm of local life.

The United Steelworkers local was, however, organized in the mid-1940s. Quiet organization was conducted by a small cadre of United Steelworkers organizers. They were joined by local leaders—called "outside" men—long employed at Cornwall. The single most important leader was Lester Yorty, who was involved in negotiating labor-management disagreements in the open pit as early as the 1920s. Yorty always had seriously questioned Bethlehem's operation at Cornwall. He was joined later by other natives of Cornwall, such as Earl Kohr, and "Red" McDaniels of Lebanon.

The strike of 1937, plus the tenuous establishment of the United Steelworkers in Cornwall, demonstrated the entrenched political position of Bethlehem Steel in Lebanon County and, particularly, in Cornwall. Bethlehem Steel employees were elected to borough and county offices at least since the consolidation of Cornwall Borough in 1926. Bethlehem managers, office workers, and other company officials served on borough council; and company management retained and exercised some influence with the county row officers as well.

The struggle over unions was also part of Bethlehem Steel's struggle to control its own future. It began losing that struggle in the 1940s and

1950s. By then much of Bethlehem's future was controlled by commodities markets, the costs of raw materials, industry-wide costs of labor, and increased competition from abroad. Especially in the 1950s, industrial activity at the mines slowed as Bethlehem Steel found it necessary to reduce costs. Ironically, by borrowing from the technology it developed at Cornwall, the corporation began to develop its mining operations in Chile and other parts of the Western Hemisphere. In other countries, where the costs of labor were cheaper, Bethlehem Steel could also experiment with new technologies beyond union restraints. By the early 1970s Cornwall was marginal, at best, and the union contract cost Bethlehem a great deal in benefits and pensions. In 1973, Bethlehem Steel closed its main Cornwall operations permanently.

LEGACIES

Nearly all the miners and their wives in Cornwall felt that the company behaved responsibly in the community and the workplace. Bethlehem Steel was responsible for all major municipal improvements, operated and kept a large stock of housing in Cornwall in repair, and initiated, with some union prodding, additional safety measures in the mines.

In the final analysis, though Bethlehem Steel bestowed these benefits on Cornwall, its presence has also retarded development in the borough. With the plant closing, not only did living standards in the borough decline, but also borough financial and environmental problems, long suppressed, came to the surface. Bethlehem Steel had paid ninety-five percent of the taxes in Cornwall and performed many civic jobs as late as the 1950s; its decision to pull out seriously eroded the tax base and curtailed essential borough services. To compensate for the loss of tax revenues the borough, over the years, had to float expensive school-bond issues. Because it did not construct an adequate sewage system when it could, the borough today faces septic-tank pollution in Toytown, Goosetown and Rexmont. In other words, it would be fair to suggest that there was inadequate preparation for the transfer from company to civic responsibility.

What is most significant about the Cornwall miners and their wives is the struggle they had to come to terms with industrialization as practiced by Bethlehem Steel. Their attitudes as workers were rooted in a concern for continuity with the past and for family and neighborhood in the present. Most often, this made for harmony in the workplace, an appreciation of past accomplishments, and an attitude of optimism for the future. Most today feel they were fortunate indeed that the Cornwall mines lasted so long and gave them and their children such a rich heritage.

9

THE SETTING

I N THE seven villages which comprised Cornwall Borough, Bethlehem Steel, until the 1960s, constructed and maintained a majority of the housing at great expense.

The area's topography conspired to isolate and thus limit the social outlook of the work force. Since new housing was built in seven villages and not scattered across the landscape, there continued a distinctive sense of neighborhood symbolized by distinctive architectural styles in each of the villages. Toytown was a prefabricated and undistinguished wood-frame housing development of the 1920s. Miner's Village and Burd-Coleman continued as distinctively limestone-constructed clusters of workers' houses. Goosetown's brick homes dominated the valley where the old roasters and anthracite furnace used to be. Rexmont was a pre-1920s Dutch settlement. North Cornwall was well known for its limestone workers' cottages. Karinchville was constructed mainly to accommodate the post World War II population boom.

The isolation of each village placed Bethlehem Steel at the center of everyday life. Let it be perfectly clear, however: Bethlehem Steel did not construct all the housing and was not involved in the manipulation of housing construction and the labor force. Most construction was a pragmatic continuation of past housing policies developed by previous companies with knowledge of the topographical limitations of the Cornwall area.

To the people who lived in the villages and worked for Bethlehem Steel's Cornwall Mines, Cornwall was, as it always had been, a closed and almost self-contained world. Most took pride in sports activities and the goings-on of the small villages. Some of the outward-looking looked forward to weekly trips to Lebanon.

Life and Labor
Before Bethlehem Steel

The interviews presented in this section convey the substance of the borough's communal memories and demonstrate the power of these memories over the lives of the working people who shared them. First, there is the narrative of the remarkable Robert Arnold, Sr., the Cornwall Railroad's agent in the borough for more than thirty-four years. His interview details the perceived *precariousness of the primary links Cornwall had with the outside world and the* seeming *permanence of the built environment in the borough. Mike Stefonich's narrative is interesting for its subtleties; it carries the conviction that the company took care of its own while at the same time it recounts the precariousness of work in the mines.*

Fairly typical of the older miners were John Yocklovich and his brother-in-law Albert Perini. Both worked at first for the Cornwall Ore Bank Company and the Robesonia Iron Company under the previous owners, the Colemans and the Freemans. These men's interviews convey a sense of continuity with the past. They served on the crews with the old ore-dumpers and haulers, the furnacemen, "buggy men" and blasters. Here they heard the stories of the old-timers, embellished them with tales of heroism and reminiscences that reflected the owners' power, and passed them along to a new generation of workers who came after the Colemans, Robesonia Iron, and the Cornwall Ore Bank Company had passed from the scene.

Coleman mansion, 1880s.

Cornwall store and meat market, Cornwall Center, late 1930s.

Robert Arnold, Sr.

Some of the building material for the Cornwall area was brought in from between Mount Gretna and Colebrook. They were going to quarry some of them stone on a larger scale, but they found out they had too much iron ore in it and it rusted. They had built a quarry but it was useless. I was agent here at Cornwall and I sent two cars to Harrisburg with the quarried stone. They only bought two carloads in Harrisburg because they found out that they had too much iron in and that they would rust. Have you often seen a house with screens where the rust was running along the building? Well, that's what this stone was doing. But now you take the Farmers Bank & Trust Company building in Lebanon—that Mann Building. The powders were made from out of Cornwall; but they had to keep them painted all the time so they wouldn't rust.

Most nearly all of them homes are sandstone from here, if you take notice. When you go down here to the school there are two homes right in across from the school. Well, them are built of sandstone. Father Coleman built a mansion right down here when you go down the road toward Quentin. Just about halfway between two homes there's a big gate. He built a great-big mansion in there of sandstone for his wife; but his wife died before it got finished and then he tore it down and then he built that church at Sixth and Chestnut Street in Lebanon right across [from] the school, catty-cornered.

But there were problems from these stones here as well. When they built the school they found that they couldn't get no corners or edge to it; so they had to get the limestone facing from Harry Millard's quarry—you know, the facing of the stone. But in the back they filled in with this stone from here. See the school, as a stone building there, is twenty-four inches wide at the walls—this limestone building. But most of the building is not made of limestone. Though Cornwall stone was not building stone, it was used to fill in.

In the early days we got all the freight for all the stores here in Lebanon County and some in from Lancaster County. They would load, say, in Philadelphia at nine o'clock and at two o'clock we would unload here at the freight office. They had about twenty-five cases for you and brought twenty-five cases for the others. They delivered for two stores in Quentin, one in Cornwall, one at Buffalo Springs, one at Schaefferstown, and two in Rexmont. Each got a shipment. The orders came around on a Tuesday and then on Thursday afternoon that stuff came over, pretty near a whole carload at a time.

We got all kinds of stuff to sell the miners. We had peaches and apples and all kinds of groceries. The molasses was in barrels, great-big barrels,

13

and then they drilled a hole in there and they put in a pump. You know you often heard, "As slow as molasses in January." Well, the bottles were outside it and in January it would kind of freeze. We got barrels of vinegar. We used to get the candy—the Easter eggs, for example, would come in great-big barrels too, 150 pounds to the barrel. On Easter each store used to get one. And we got fresh peaches at that time. Pretty near all the dry food came in containers, twenty-five pounds to a container—prunes, peaches, apricots, raisins, and all of that. And then they would just open them and they would weigh it out about a pound at a time. See, everybody had to get it there. At that time there wasn't much travel.

Most of the people did their shopping here and stayed here. You did all your shopping in the Cornwall Store. Buffalo Springs, you done pretty near all your shopping there; Buffalo Springs is between Cornwall and Schaefferstown. And Schaefferstown has a store. They have one yet, Umberger's Store. If you go down there yet, that's the way those kind of stores were. The Cornwall Ore Bank Company owned only the one in Miner's Village. The others were all owned by individuals. Of course, now the Cornwall Store had a post office right in it. Whoever was handling the store had to take the post office because it was built right in the store. They had a book. They had thousands of dollars that they didn't get paid because people didn't pay. Say you went in there and you had a book and if you bought a loaf of bread, they would put on a loaf of bread, four cents. Then they would mark that on your pile and then about once a week or so you would go over and pay your bill. You didn't carry money along when you went over to the store.

Bethlehem Steel only came in in October, 1916. Then they bought out the Lackawanna Iron and Steel furnaces—two furnaces. And then the next year they bought the Lebanon Steel in Lebanon in 1917. Then in 1923 they bought the mines. Last they bought Robesonia. Robesonia was down there near Reading and had a share here in the Cornwall Ore Banks. The Ore Bank Company had ore here at Cornwall; Robesonia had a furnace at Robesonia. Every day they would send seven ore cars here empty and they would return to the Robesonia to run their furnaces. Their agreement with the Colemans read they could get ore "as long as water runs and grass grows." Robesonia dug out enough ore to run the furnace. Then back in 1926 Bethlehem Steel bought the furnace at Robesonia and then a year after that they tore it down. Then Bethlehem came back and bought the pits from the Freemans for a million dollars, and then they had the whole business.

The main reason for having the railroads was to bring the iron ore to Lebanon. When they opened up first they hauled ore from the Cornwall

14

Mines in by vans to the Union Canal there at Eleventh and Canal in Lebanon. And then they loaded it on a canal boat to send it up to Steelton to the furnace. The boats went up the canal. The canal went from the Schuylkill River in Reading to the Susquehanna River in Middletown. Then they sent that up on boats to Middletown and then from Middletown they went up the Susquehanna River to Steelton with the ore. In 1854 they built the Cornwall Railroad, and then in 1858 they built the Reading Railroad and then after that the canal stopped.

Later Bethlehem Steel leased the railroads from the Coleman interests, but then later on Bethlehem Steel bought the railroads. When they bought the mines then they bought the railroad. Bethlehem Steel bought it from what they called the Cornwall Estate. Then Bethlehem Steel had the railroads and the mines.

Mike Stefonich

The Cornwall store was the company store for all of the surrounding area. This was back at the turn of the century. The people told me this. I didn't know about it in my time. But then the Cornwall Ore Bank people didn't have to pay you money; but you could go to the Cornwall store and get food on the book. Over at the mill you could get feed for your animals if you had chickens, or cows or what have you. The first of May they would have what you call Draw Day. And they would balance their books, and if you owed them money, that would kind of stay on the account. If they owed you money, they paid you what they had to. I never experienced that. This is hearsay, what I'm giving you right now. But the old-timers would tell me about this Drawing Day business.

Then my father worked at the furnace. My father was not a mine employee. He may have been before I knew. But my father, when I knew him, worked at the furnace. Like I tell you, he was a furnace boss, a roaster boss, and he took care of the roaster as I remember him. And he worked at the furnace. And the furnaces were dismantled around 1921 or '22. Then he may have worked up at the mines until '25. I think he did in that area. By that time he was an old man. He worked until the year he died. He died at the age of 71; there were no pensions then, yet. And he used to go around opening ditches so water wouldn't collect. That's what he did till the year he died.

In his better years the furnace was the place to work because the risks weren't so great. They didn't do blasting or shooting there. There's always danger of drilling into dynamite that didn't go off before. They thought it did but you couldn't tell. When you shot it off, they had blue marks in their skin where they had powder burns.

North Cornwall blast furnace producing "pigs," late 1800s.

I used to see them put these charges off at first. They were all fuses and a fellow would go with a tape or something like this and light these fuses or cords, they call them, I guess. They had a three-foot length and it would take them two minutes to burn. And this fellow had two minutes to light all these charges before the thing went off. He did it in such a way that he got the harder ones first and the easiest ones last, and then he hid back of the shovel. That was the protection; the shovel was made of sheet iron and stuff like that and was in the vicinity. The big blast, of course, was an electric charge that you had wires on and you pressed the thing and it all went off in one bam.

Albert Perini

I worked for Robesonia before Bethlehem bought in. When I worked for Robesonia I didn't need anything; they didn't bother too much with papers. I was going to school and they came back and asked my father if

16

he would go over to them; they needed a blaster. See, anybody couldn't blast at that time and my father could. Then my father said, "Yes, if you give my boy a job." Then the superintendent said, "How old is he?" My pop said, "Sixteen." "O.K., he can carry water." At that time you had to carry water. So I started there and I worked there until, I think it was about '28, till Bethlehem Steel bought them over. Then I worked at Bethlehem Steel a little while. That's when Mike Stefonich come and ask me, "Albert, you're not eighteen." I said, "Yes, I am." He said, "You'll need a paper. Your daddy got to swear, or you need a paper." "Well," I said, "My daddy will swear. Don't worry about that." Then that's when we went to the principal and got a paper that night.

I always carried water for the men at Robesonia. I carried water for so long. Then I got to be tool boy and carried the steel down in the pit for the men to use in the drills. At that time they drug it—it was eighteen-foot steel. I started at two footer and then four, six, eight, ten, twelve, fourteen, sixteen and kept going on like that. I had to carry them up the steps. You run the drill by air, you know. Two men would work on it, and one guy would stand up high. There was a lever on top. You turned this lever. Well, you had to know how to turn it, not force it. After you worked it for a while, hell, you could easy operate it. You know how to operate it. And they would put powder in there and blasted it. I carried steel for it a while. These drills were smaller ones. And then I was on that for a while and then a job opened up in the blacksmith shop. Then I got to be a blacksmith helper.

Then one day the superintendent came in to me—I was just turning eighteen—and he said, "Albert, next week or maybe by the end of the month I'm going to send you down on the shovel." We had steam shovels at that time that were operated by firemen. "I want you to learn to be a fireman; you're young. Then I'm going to break you in to run the shovel, because you're young." I said, "O.K." And in a month's time Robesonia sold out—in 1928. Goodbye. Hello, Bethlehem Steel.

I liked being waterboy best. There were forty-five men working there. And I had to carry water for the forty-five men with that yolk on my back and two buckets of water. I had to go up to the spring. We had a good spring up there—that was ice-cold water. I had to come down; there was 225 steps to go down. I had to go down and come up eighteen times a day. They had railings on each side of the steps and this skip would go up and down outside—pass you. You had to watch to keep your bucket in. Then sometimes when I had to go down after them, according to who was looking, I would put my feet on these two railings, you know, and slide down. I tell you, it wasn't easy for us, but we thought it was alright.

17

North Cornwall furnace, 1917.

John Yocklovich

These old timers got to talking about blast furnaces recently. One asked me where I lived first. I said, "Cornwall." "Oh! I know a little history of Cornwall." I said, "You do?" "Yeah, about the blast furnaces. We heard about the Anthracite." And then he said something about one of the girls [one of the daughters of the Colemans, the owners before Bethlehem Steel and Lackawanna]. She wanted a furnace, so they went and built a furnace at Burd-Coleman. They made two of them over there and, eventually, another party—I don't know who it was—said they wanted a furnace. So they built one out at North Cornwall. There was the old anthracite furnace. Then in Colebrook there was one. They had one in North Lebanon, too. The Colemans and the Freemans owned all of it; they were interrelated. So, in other words, they had five furnaces here then.

They tore this one down here at Anthracite, finally, you know. The way I understand it was—I got my information from old Joe Donnaly. See, he was a watchman; he got hurt over in the mines. See, Lackawanna owned furnaces—the blast furnaces—before Bethlehem Steel bought it. I remember that. When the people worked for them they were very good to them. Every so many years they tore the lining out, and then the men would be off of work maybe for a couple of months. Then they would get them to work down here in the creek, to straighten out the creek; they would use pick and shovel and cart. This was so they wouldn't be out of work. But, anyhow, I talked to this old guy and I said, "I even pulled buggies." He looked at me, "Aw!" Well, all of these big, strapping guys and me, a little midget then.

For ore and stone you had to use a small buggy, see. Even in small buggies the weight was there. A coke buggy was bigger. You had to load your buggies; if you overload it too much on your hands, well, you can hardly lift it up. You had to load it right in the center. I know. I hate to brag now but I was just as good at that as anyone. We worked like mules, you better believe it; there was six of us in all. We had so many buggies of coke, so many buggies of ore; we used to pull two buggies of Port Emory ore and one buggy of Cornwall. We'd go to the roasters. You know, the roasters are right there in the back where they roasted our Cornwall ore to get the sulphur out of it. They got it red hot. When we took it to the furnaces it came out just like a buttermilk, when you make butter. Then they have a hole in the side with a runner and they run that iron into great-big laddles. Years ago that used to be a sight for the people to see. When they dumped that slag, you know you could see it clean into Lebanon; red-hot cinder would light up the sky. And the lower part where the iron come out was about eight feet lower. They run that out into what they called a bed. This was all sand out here. They had patterns. They were something like that [he measures about a foot high with his hands] and I would say about three foot long. The colored fellows used to carry that. They would have a little cart loaded up like cordwood and take it out on the cart and pile it on the car. They would take it down here to Lebanon and pile it up. They was smart. It would depend how the stock market was. [Laughs.] The stock market went up, they sold the iron; if it was down, they kept it for themself. But they would send it to the furnaces for open-hearth use. They were really smart; that's where they made their millions of dollars.

I worked with my dad; we were buddies. He'd give me the devil. He'd say, "Why did you take that job? You won't be able to do that! You'll play out." Heck, I used to have fun with them buggies. See, before I used to sweep and when the men carried buggies they dropped their coke. I would sweep it under the chutes. I thought, "Well, I can do this, too." That's how I learned.

Poor old John Falk! He was a great-big, powerful man around over two hundred and some pounds. I used to pity them. He said, "You little bugger, you! How in the hell can you do it and I can't do it?" I said, "It's just a knack, John." He carried his. I used to pity him. His arms would get so tired. He was a great-big red-haired guy about six foot two. That's how I got to know Falky, then.

19

Buggy crew at North Cornwall, ca. 1910, John Yocklovich's father on left.

The People: The Dutch,
The Newcomers and the Engineers

The turn-of-the-century labor force of the Cornwall area was predominantly Pennsylvania German, or Dutch, whose ancestors had migrated from the Palatinate region of Germany in the mid-eighteenth century. Even in the early twentieth century they retained many of the characteristics of their forebears—love of lots of good food, thriftiness ("tightness" most outsiders called it), loyalty to employers, industriousness, a bit of backwardness, but not poverty. All of these characteristics are reflected in the interviews with Lester Yorty, Hilda Stahley Perini and Robert Arnold, Sr. Just as Lester Yorty loved to talk about his romance with food, Hilda Perini dwelled at length on the preparation and preservation of various traditional Dutch foods. Both interviews give substance to the phrase "self-sufficiency."

The memories of the foreign-born and their children were not entirely pleasant. They dwelled on struggle and survival in the old country and the new. Mike Stefonich's and Peter Rossini's memoirs deal particularly well with the living conditions in Cornwall, the rough housing available to newcomers, the crowding in the small villages, the boarders taken in, and some of the discontent. The burdens were bearable, however, when compared to the conditions in the old country or, in the case of Peter Rossini, Jr., to the cold and isolation of the Mesabi Iron Range in Minnesota, where his "Pop" first worked.

The foreign-born rapidly settled into Cornwall, however. Strengthening their customs from the old country was the knowledge the newcomers gleaned from the Dutch: survival depended on family, community-wide celebrations, the preparation of food and clothing, and the exchange of and barter for necessities in a non-monetary economy. Life was precarious and options were few. Mike Stefonich's, Matt "Tip" Karinch's and Peter Rossini, Jr.'s interviews all convey this sense of the precariousness of life.

Other feelings co-existed with the values of scarcity. The foreign-born appear to have been more robust, and dreamed up many occasions on which to be convivial. Albert Perini's and Mike Stefonich's marvelous interviews detail the foreign-born's many celebrations.

Black migrants to Cornwall from southern states never intended to stay. The Lackawanna Steel Company and Bethlehem Steel recruited Afro-Americans from the South. Though their efforts were somewhat

21

successful, the great majority of blacks returned to the South. Those who stayed began in the most dangerous positions, on the blasting crews and as timbermen, and a few of them, such as Jack Jordan, eventually became foremen. Mrs. Warner Franklin's interview gives some indication of how racial prejudice broke down.

Another element working in Cornwall, but seldom written about, was the old non-Dutch working class which migrated from the anthracite counties of Pennsylvania. Russell "Red" McDaniels' interview portrays the nature of these working-class neighborhoods on "the wrong side of the tracks" in Lebanon City. Most of these men made friends with the foreign-born and the "colored" workers. Cornwall represented a chance to climb out of their cycle of poverty and repression.

Inhabiting an entirely different world were Cornwall's first mining engineers and their wives, brought in by Bethlehem Steel in the late 1920s and the 1930s. To these people, especially the wives, the most noticeable things about Cornwall were its isolation and the absence of other professional families. Lebanon City was little better; it was rough, backward and clannish.

The catalyst of the growth of the engineering population was World War II, when Bethlehem Steel expanded its facilities in Lebanon and began to experiment with metallurgy and cobalt for the United States government. It became more apparent that the workers and engineers/professionals dwelled in separate spheres. Mrs. P. L. Steffensen's interview is rich with the descriptions of coffee klatches, buffets, poker parties, picnics and P.T.A. meetings; members of this circle were divided between Toytown and Karinchville, whereas most of the workers lived in Burd-Coleman, Miner's Village, Goosetown and Rexmont.

THE DUTCH

Robert Arnold, Sr.

I was born in 1891. We moved up there to Millard's near Annville in 1892. We moved away from there in 1898; we lived there six years on the Millard Farm. Then we moved down to Martin's Grocery Store—is below Annville, right there at that farm. We built there and my father died there in 1912 and my mother in 1925. In 1910 I graduated from the Institute of Telegraphy in Lebanon. After graduation I went to New York on the Erie Railroad. I worked there for six years. Then there was an opening at the Cornwall-Lebanon Railroad. And then I came up here and I worked there for thirteen months, from March 1, 1916 to March 31, 1917. Then I transferred from there to the Cornwall Railroad. In 1918 Cornwall-Lebanon sold out to the Pennsylvania. Then there was no Cornwall-Lebanon anymore; then it didn't take long till the agents at Cornwall were at some other place. So if I wouldn't have changed, I would've got out of Cornwall. So I went in to the Lebanon-Donaghmore station in Lebanon for two years as carrier clerk for the Cornwall Railroad. Back in 1918 the government took over all the railroads, during the First World War. Anybody that worked on the railroad worked the same as if he worked for the government. That happened in June of 1918. The first of that month an army officer, Captain A. M. Patton, came. He

Lebanon-Donaghmore station, Cornwall Railroad, 1920.

23

was a Civil War captain and he had lost his legs. So he was manager; he hired me on the first of June, 1918, as an agent at Cornwall. I was there until 1950 when they closed that station.

Lester Yorty

My date of birth was April 20, 1903, and I was born in the town of Annville. I then went to Elizabethtown with my family for about two years. My dad was a shoe cutter after he came off the farm. His sisters and brothers had farms; he often went and helped out with them. He was the youngest of the family. I think he had thirteen brothers and sisters. His parents originally came from Grantham, where they farmed around two hundred acres or something like that. At home we ate meat and potatoes mostly. Usually we had a one-course meal, like pot roast and potatoes and carrots and onions. Then my grandmother would lay the cookies here, and the pie, and another pie here and another kind of cookies on a big, long table. I swear I became a Pennsylvania Dutch cookie and pie eater. [Laughs.] But some of the things I ate there! I didn't realize it at the time that we didn't have the money to buy candy at that time. My people made root beer, or ginger ale or something like that; they made it to sell. That's the way we got it. Ice cream was usually homemade, but the only time you got it was maybe the Fourth of July and Labor Day, or something like that—a special occasion. You didn't get ice cream like that; they made it to sell.

My grandfather was hardworking, and every penny he earned they'd eat it. He had a fixed rule—he didn't object if you went and cleaned your plate and you went for second helpings. It was there; he didn't object to that. We were always taught, you ate according to the quantity that was in front of you. You didn't go and dig out a big piece of what's-its-name and put it on your plate when you had brothers and sisters. You knew if you dug out that portion they wouldn't have any. You tried to divide it up. In fact, sometimes they would cut it up into portions. But the one thing I often remember and can appreciate is that the old fellow worked hard for his money. He said, "Don't let your eyes be bigger than your stomach." In other words, if you're hungry and the food is there, and there is some left and the others have eaten, take it. He didn't begrudge you that. But he did hate waste because he had to work so hard to put it on the table. Now my father liked to drink a little bit; he liked to play cards and things like that. I don't know why he drank or what he was really looking for, but I'm sure he didn't find it. Towards the end he used to try to get my brother and I to come down and take his insurance business because he couldn't handle it. He couldn't see right towards the

24

end. My daddy felt that life owes you a living but you better be sure to go out and collect it. This is a little different than some people feel; they think life owes you something.

My mother got us out on Sunday. In Elizabethtown, when I went to Sunday School—when I would walk down on Brown Street to go to Sunday School—it was according to which neighbor I met along the way that dictated which Sunday School I went to. So I had no preference in church. I believed in the House of God whether it's a different denomination, or a different religion. If it's God's, it should be respected by all people, not just the church ones. I guess I went to everyone's Sunday School in Elizabethtown at one time or another. [Laughs.] It doesn't matter to me what makes one church better than the other. My mother was concerned only that I went to Sunday School.

You know, I used to wonder when I went to the Annville Sunday School why the people used to hum when they were supposed to sing hymns. I used to often wonder why they would hum. At that age I didn't know how to read and write. I wasn't going to school at that time that they would hum. In later years, I found out that early in the time a lot of people didn't know how to read and write, but they could hum to a melody or tune. So they would hum instead. This was United Brethren. The fact is—I heard that thought given out—that people in those days didn't know how to read and write. But they did know the tune from handing down from one generation to another—"Onward Christian Soldiers," "The Old Rugged Cross," you know.

I got in trouble if I kicked the bucket around the house or maybe gave back-talk or something; I got a whack. One instance I always liked to save. My parents had just got me a pair of corduroy pants with a lining in them. That was the thing—you know the midriff-like pants with a lining in. My mother must have said something to me and she gave me a whack. And I just said, "Ha, ha, that didn't hurt." She came running after me. We had a little horse and buggy stable up at the end of the lot there. I went and hid the ladder and went in the loft and she couldn't follow me. But sooner or later, you know, you get hungry and you come in to eat. When I came in for supper she took them corduroy pants down and she gave it to me, and I couldn't say "Ha, ha" then. [Laughs.]

I got married because I got trapped. My Dutch heritage made me like food too much. My wife-to-be's mother knew that. After I met her at a ball game she said, "Go back and invite Lester over for supper." So her mother made what I called "smashed" potatoes. When I ate and we had smashed potatoes and sauerkraut, I'd fill my plate up and eat! Her mother said, "The next time Lester comes over we'd better cut more potatoes." [Laughs for a while.] I had a good appetite. Like I say, I was very active so I burned it up. I got married about a year after that. I had not saved up too much money. We *must* have lived with her parents for more than six years! And our oldest son was born in 1925. We moved here in March of '32 to this house in Toytown. This house was built in 1926. See, these homes were built in 1927.

We've been very fortunate. I've told fellows that came in here when we had a coal-oil stove how fortunate we've been. This fellow wanted to sell me a heater—electric or gas. I think it was electric. And he said, "You know, Mr. Dougherty and Mr. Peterson [the Bethlehem mine superintendents] had one." I looked at him and I said, "Look, Mr. Dougherty and Mr. Peterson can buy and sell me. I ain't keeping up with the Joneses. The best thing you can do is leave right now and head for that door." I chased him out; I don't believe in that. So we've been fortunate; we're satisfied. Our wants and wishes haven't been that great so we don't owe anyone anything in current bills.

Mrs. Hilda Stahley Perini

My mother worked in the mill all her life, William H. Noggle & Sons. They made underwear. I'll tell you something that you don't know about. They made union suits for men years ago. I was twelve when I worked during the summer. I sewed on buttons after school. I would come home from high school on the bus and jump off the bus and go to work for two hours. I earned nice money.

We always knew how to work. There was many a load of wood; I helped to carry it in when it was chopped by my uncle. He would chop it and we would rack it up for the wintertime. Then in the fall when you got twenty-five bushels of potatoes and the coal bin was filled—boy we were rich. That's all you needed for the wintertime. My grandmother would do all the jarring and all the canning and she would be making jams; we never went hungry. We had a big garden. Oh, how I dreaded that big garden. We grew everything! Sweet potatoes, corn, carrots, beets, peas, potatoes, etc.!!

As I got older I would help to clean and cook. My grandmother did all the cooking. Saturday my aunt would bake, my mother and I would clean, and my grandmother would cook. I'll tell you how my aunt baked. Everything had to be there. And by grandma would bake every Saturday morning a coconut-custard pie. She would have one crock full of eggs and another crock full of flour. Everything was right there and she never measured anything, and I would say, "How do you do that?" "Just like this." I make it but it wasn't hers.

On Thanksgiving my mother bought a turkey for $25. In those days

Noggle's shirt factory, Rexmont; closed 1978.

you didn't have turkeys like you do now. You'd have seven sweets and seven sours. That's Pennsylvania Dutch! Well, that would be cookies, pies, etc. Then you have your pickles and your preserved green beans—those were done up sour—or cucumber salad with sour cream on it. Seven sweets and seven sours! You'd have cranberry sauce and each one got a glass of wine and a great-big serving of turkey. The wood stove did it all—cook, heat water and roast the turkey. The kitchen filled with the smell of good food.

Every Saturday morning she would bake and make potpie while she was baking. The meat would be cooking on the stove at the same time. And she would make a great-big kettle of potpie. I think we ate a bushel of it in one year.

At Eastertime my mother would make candy—which I never cared for. She would get the coconuts and grind it and make the candy and then coat it. Now that was about three days' work. She had enough for everybody. I never had any kids to play with but there were ten at Albert's [future husband's] house. At Eastertime they always waited for the baked-ham sandwiches. But I would sneak some and would chop some baked ham off and take it out to them. At Easter they couldn't wait for the candy. Since I didn't eat mine I just gave it to them. And she would make enough sand tarts at Christmastime to fill a large lard can. Also, she made ginger snaps and the sugar cookies.

You sat up and ate everything on your plate. My grandma always said she never saw anyone eat sauerkraut soup like I did. I like the mashed potatoes with just the broth. We ate it all because we didn't know any better; it was there and everything was in season and you had no choice.

We had all the conveniences of a large city. The greengrocer would come by in a horse and wagon. The baker, Mr. Oltenburstel, a German whom we could barely understand, had a bakery there. When they would come back from the bakery, those buns would be warm when we got them. Then the butcher would come in his wagon. He'd blow his horn; you'd go out and pick out your meat. The greengrocer would come and you would go out and pick up fruit out of season. You know in seventy-five years this is the first time that I can remember that there are no mills and stores. We used to have two mills and two or three or four stores and now we don't have a one. That's one thing we miss.

We made our own clothes. My aunt made many of my clothes. I had beautiful clothes. And at Eastertime I would have my white kid shoes and white gloves. At Christmastime I always got pretty dresses. My doll, that my daughter has, is dressed similar to the one that I had at one time. And I remember a beautiful new sapphire-blue velvet dress I got when I was older.

I learned how to sew myself one day. My mother sewed in the mill every day. Every Saturday night I thought I had to have a new dress just to walk up the street. And I would stop by the grocery store and buy material. You could buy all the material you wanted besides the groceries. I would pick a piece of material up, bring it home, and she would make me a dress—no questions asked. So this one time I had gone over to Lebanon and I came home with a piece of white linen. Everybody was wearing a white linen dress. Well, she was in no mood to make a dress that Saturday. She said, "Get the pattern out and get a big table to cut it out." Well, I cried a little bit but decided I might as well start. I did make the dress and from then on I sewed.

I couldn't talk about anything with my mother. The Pennsylvania Dutch didn't do that. We didn't understand a lot of the gossip. We weren't suppose to know. Things like that were never brought up at the table. You never brought your work up or the gossip—that was out, that was besides the point. We had to mind our own business; we had to behave. Otherwise you would get a smack.

In those days before Bethlehem Steel, we didn't have a telephone; we didn't have buses; we didn't have any communication. The only communication was by mail. We didn't have anything. Where did you go? We didn't travel. You don't know anything like that, but we had no communication at that time.

Our relatives from Reading would drop a card; you saw the cards.

28

They would be up on Sunday. Well, that meant that my grandmother and the whole gang of us at home—my aunts and everybody else— would have a big dinner. All the company would be sitting on the front porch in Cornwall all dressed up. My grandma and her three sisters were Pennsylvania Dutch. They'd talk and gossip in Dutch then. There would be a Packard sitting in front of the house; it was one made to order, too, the way they wanted it. And Aunt Jane wore all the hats that were custom-made; she had a custom-made Packard and a custom-made hat. Then she had black help in Reading in a mansion house. They owned the Engle Hotel in town [Lebanon].

This was a nice community. We had nice people. We could never say anything bad. Then Bethlehem Steel came in and they did the highways for us; and they brought the water in. The Metropolitan [Edison Electric] came in with the lights; we didn't have lights before, you know. We had coal-oil lamps, or kerosene lamps. You would have one thunderstorm and you had no lights. With the early electric there was little improvement. It was early equipment and it wasn't up to snuff.

Stahley family on a Sunday afternoon, early 1930s; Albert Perini on right.

NEWCOMERS

Robert Arnold, Sr.

In 1916, December, they brought a hundred colored people from the South to work for the mines. They came in here on 1916, December 4, near where I was working at the Cornwall Station. They got off about four o'clock and they had a little snow. They never seen snow and they didn't like it. Then about one-third went over to the Rexmont Hotel; the other one-third went to the Quentin Hotel; and the other one-third went to the Bluebird. They stayed overnight and then they went home. If they would've stayed two months, then they would've paid their transportation; but a whole lot went home that didn't want to stay. Some stayed here the year around and when they died here they were buried back in their hometown in the South where they were born. Some lived in Burd-Coleman. There was Al Brisbaine, Irvin Lee, Robert Roberts, and Warner Franklin was here then too. He came up then in 1916. Mr. Franklin's widow is still around Cornwall. They were all hired in here for the Bethlehem mines.

Now there were foreign-born who came to work in the mines. Rossinis came over from Italy and they were the miners; and they hired them to work in the mines—to undermine the mines, because the Bethlehem people didn't know how to undermine them. Rossini came to be the head man. Then he taught all these others how to mine underground.

Superintendent Peterson came around 1920—in that neighborhood. When he came here, he just came on a cart and he had ragged clothing on and all. He didn't have to move in the mansion; he moved in another house and he told me he was so glad because the mansion cost $75 more a month. And $75 looked good to him. And he told stories. We found out he made around $190,000. But he only had $95,000 take-home money. And when I came home my wife said, "Only $95,000 take-home money for a year. There's a book!"

Albert Perini

My father came from Italy to Cornwall. My mother was born in Italy too, but not her sisters. She lived there until, I guess, my daddy got in with her. There was another fellow there. This other guy came over here with my pop too, an Italian guy. Then this one fella said to my pop, "Hey, make a date with that woman for me, will you?" My pop said, "O.K." Instead of making a date for him, my pop made a date for himself and then he got married to my mom. [Laughs.]

30

No. 9 steam shovel and crew in the open pit, 1930s; Albert Perini's father is on the right.

Now when my dad worked here, he worked outside all the time in the open pit. Then they got the Spaniards [Mexicans] here. There was some Spaniards who came here. My pop could talk to them. That's what they enjoyed. My pop could talk to Italians and he could talk to Spanish and he could talk a lot of Dutch.

My father always talked about Rome since he came from around Rome. My pop, Paul Perini, landed in New York, and then his brother was there in New York. He only had one brother. Them New York and New Jersey people were glad [to visit] here because I was born right out there in Rexmont. You see, there were little towns right here in Cornwall. That was the same thing as in the old country. Over there they had little towns here and there. Well, the people stuck together here a little more than in New York. See, in the old days the Italians or the hunkies or whatever you want to call them, they stuck together to help one another out. That's what made this country, too. You better believe it!

Along with ten children we had boarders—maybe three, four or five of them. When they come from the foreign countries they would always come to my mom's. You see, my mother wrote and spoke Italian. She was the only woman around here that could write Italian. She was an in-

31

terpreter. She could write Italian better than these people that would write Italian in Italy and send them over here. Then my mother had to read letters from the old country to them. And my mother went to court when they had to have an Italian interpreter to talk; she done that.

And boy, could those newcomers sing! When they drank beer [after work] they would start singing. My pop and my uncle were good singers too. My pop would be singing all the time. When he would go to work in the morning at six o'clock, he would take off and you could hear him whistling or singing going down the street. At that time they walked everywhere—they always walked everywhere, and they always walked to work. They didn't have anything, and raising ten kids in those days was a problem.

When I got married (April 29, 1929) these priests were as strict as hell, you know. My wife wasn't Catholic so I went down to the Father and said, "Can you marry me next Monday night?" "What do you mean, next Monday night?" I said, "In the house." "Oh," he said, "we don't marry in the house." They didn't. I said, "Could you marry me?" And he said, "Yes." Then I went to work and I came home Thursday night and my mom said, "Father Martin called. He wants to see you." I went down and said, "What do you want, Father?" "I can't marry you in the house Monday night." "Why not?" "Oh, the Pope so and so." I said, "You tell the Pope, O.K, I'll go out here with her and get married." The Methodist Church was over there. "I'll go over there." "Oh no, no, don't. Come on down anyway." And we got married on a Monday night. He didn't want to marry us in the house. After we got married we went into my uncle's store in Lebanon. My grandmother wanted to see us. And we bought some ham and cake and stuff and we came out to my mother's in Cornwall and we had a little lunch. We slept at my sister's that night and the next day the furniture came and we went to housekeeping at the Brick Row [old company homes]. We paid nine dollars a month.

It was rough at first in the Row. We didn't like it. You didn't have no water or nothing. They had a little bell outside. If you didn't get up early in the morning you didn't get no water. You had to pump it. One pump for all the people. And the toilets out back were double. We had new furniture, that's all. Anyways, that was in May. We lived there about five months.

And then a man had this home in Rexmont all done over and we bought it and moved in in November. My, how people would peep in the windows. You know, the open stairway and all. They thought we was millionaires then. That part back there [the kitchen] wasn't on it then. Just this one room here, and then we had a little room next to it on the first floor. The bathroom wasn't here and that back part there was nothing, just a little porch there. This is one of the oldest houses around.

After we lived here for a while we finally put the bathroom in. Me and this one foreman put it in ourself. I had a hell of a time getting the lumber. You had to do so much running around to find it. And me and him did everything but a little bit of the plumbing work and the plastering. I dug that cellar out by hand. There was a lot of stones and everything and we done everything. I had some help. The one foreman that worked with me up here helped. I would help him to repair his house. He had an old house and we repaired his. Then he helped me to repair mine. He was a good carpenter.

We made a living because my wife's mother helped us. We didn't even own a newspaper. My wife's grandma would go to the butcher wagon and buy meat for us all. Well, she was a good cook and she needed some things and she always brought them to us. Just about the time the butcher went down the street, you would see her coming up the back way to our place with some meat under her apron. And she would say to me that we needed some meat. We also ate ducks, too. I believe we ate fifty ducks one winter. Her mother raised ducks. Oh, we had ducks down there!! The mothers would lay the eggs and they would get to hatching. Some morning you would get up and the old duck would come out with about fifteen young ones.

Then we had front-door service. Some of them hucksters would blow their horn and you would know they were there. They had a fruit man that would come—bananas, oranges and apples. The baker would come along; the baker had a truck and would go around with the bread. His name was old Altenburster. He was German. They had a baker shop. I'm telling you, when those buns came down the street they were hot in the wagon and were they good, wow! He was an old guy that ran a store and he would have a man come out every morning from Lebanon to do the baking—Joe Faggan his name was. He would do the baking and bread and stuff. He made the big sugar cookies.

Mike Stefonich

Before Bethlehem Steel, Cornwall was like a barony. The people were all serfs. You have to go back to the beginning. To start off with—the mine started with a fellow named Grubb—Peter Grubb. He in turn had a granddaughter that married a fellow by the name of Coleman who was an iron person—knew the iron business from over in England. Then there were the Colemans, three generations of them over here, and they married into the Freemans. This Mr. Freeman, over here in the 1880s-

33

1890s, was the last of them. And he owned the mansion where the present Methodist home is. And they still owned this land across the Cornwall Road here. They were the people who kept this like a serfdom. I remember when I was a little child that my father told my mother, "The wage was a dollar and a half a day under the Colemans." You see, you worked twelve-hour shifts at the furnace. It was the best wages he ever got up at that time. Get that, a dollar and a half a day! Lord, he raised nine kids on that! I was born in 1902, my youngest brother was born in 1918. So it wasn't all at once.

My mother used to tell me we used to live in what they called a shanty in Burd-Coleman. Now, you wouldn't believe this, but we had private living quarters for my father and the family and so on. Then there was like an addition on the house with all beds in it—wooden beds with straw mattresses. My mother told me she kept as a young woman *twenty-four* boarders; there, get that, *twenty-four boarders*! And she had one colored woman coming in to help her with the wash and things. And she fed these men and looked after them. For that she would get twenty dollars a month. And that's how my father and mother started housekeeping.

My father come over in 1893 from what today would be Yugoslavia. Then it was Austria-Hungary. My father served in the Austrian army. My father was what you'd call a peddler today. But you have to give it its proper perspective. Over in Europe, you didn't have these notion stores and these things. My father would have a horse and buggy and he would have a trunk packed with needles and thread and other various notions which the various people in the communities would need. There weren't any stores like there are today. My father made a living like that over there. He didn't tell me too much about this. But, anyway, he came over to this country and then he became a day laborer here.

You must get my father's life in its proper perspective of why he came. When I worked up at the mines in 1926 we had a fellow—a very intelligent fellow—from the old country. Over in Europe they had conscription—you had to serve in the army when you became eighteen. But this fellow—this was a friend of my father's—snuck away when he was seventeen. There was an agent of the steel company over there recruiting people for work over here. And they paid your fare and food and found you quarters over here. And then you refunded your fare after you worked here. They conscripted people in Europe. Foreign-born wanted to get out—they had to!! It was your Polish up in the Coal Region, it was your Slovenes in Steelton here who left Europe to build America.

My mother come over from the old country with four women. My mother told me she worked two years to save $48 to come to this country. Two years till she had that saved! She landed in Baltimore [laughs] and so she was met by her stepmother. (I didn't even tell this to my children, but my grandfather, after my mother was born, lost his wife. Then he married a second time. You had to marry again because over in Europe both husband and wife worked in the field. You just can't make it otherwise. Then my grandfather married again. And then they had this woman who would have been my mother's stepmother; then my grandfather passed away. She must have been a young woman. I never met the woman, by the way. She passed away before I was aware what the score was.) My mother's stepmother met her in Baltimore and brought her to Reading. My mother used to say that she got a job working for some Jewish fellow as a domestic. And my mother worked as a maidservant and that's where she met my father. My father came from Cornwall. Then these people would get together in Reading and my mother's stepmother arranged for my mother to marry my father. This is around 1900 [1901].

At that time there's a large Slovenian population in Reading down around Railroad Street and Schuylkill Avenue, and in along that area. The reason I'm familiar with it is because after the depression hit us in 1918—after I got out of high school—well, I went to Reading to work. My parents met in Reading and got married and moved to Cornwall, and lived over at first in Burd-Coleman. Today, it's called Iron Master's Row now. Back then it was called Hunkytown. The village right next to us was Dutchtown. Goosetown was again our class of people. Rexmont was a gang of people who were here for more than one or two generations ahead of us. Miner's Village again was a new community. That was built

Burd-Coleman, a workers' village, 1925.

35

in 1870; it was the first house that was built up there. The reason they built that was that up until that time people drifted in and drifted out because they had no place to stay. When those houses were built, one family was downstairs and one family was upstairs. They had three rooms, no bathroom. You only had outhouses. We had outhouses here, oh, I'd say until about 1930, in Cornwall Borough. There were no toilets, except superintendents' houses. Toytown was the first community that had bathroom facilities. Back in Hunkytown we lived in shanties on the north side of the road. New homes are being built on the south side of the same road where I used to roam as a kid. I went down to this little red schoolhouse, across from the limestone schoolhouse. I never went to the limestone school.

In those days, as a rule, the foreign-born people had the labor jobs. The people who were natives generally were mechanics and locomotive engineers, and things that required a little more intelligence. My father was a shovel pusher, a wheelbarrow pusher. Ha-ha. When I started work, I unloaded cinders from the furnace and picked out metals. That was during the war in 1918 when I was only sixteen, so I wasn't allowed to work in the furnace. But they gave me a job of unloading a scrap car out of the cinder bank. By that time I was carrying newspapers. Then the boss, a fellow by the name of Fisher, would come there in the afternoon and he and I would sit under the car and read the paper. After that I worked in a textile mill, E. Richard Meinig, for about two years. And then the bottom dropped out of the silk market and all the single men had to leave. There was only single shift then. I, being single at the time, was left go, which was all right for me. Up until I got the job at Bethlehem Steel I never held a job more than two years. So that was part of the way things went.

You must realize why this way of life seemed so good. You must compare it to the home country. My parents came from Yugoslavia, from my ancestors' village, called Mala-Lycha, which means "little woods." In 1938, when I went to Mala-Lycha, I met my mother's sister and I'll never forget. I gave her ten dollars, and she was so happy; she had ten American dollars. She was going to buy her winter clothing with that.

I met a man over there who had worked here while I was a timekeeper in the mines. And he had returned to the old country and he recognized me and I spent some time with him. He lived in a stone house and his barn was cemented right up against his house, and the manure pile was between the house and the barn. And that provided heat for his place. That *decaying* manure! Can you believe it or not?! And they lived like that! And this is how my folks lived over there. You had to see this to know what living conditions were like in those times.

36

My parents taught me the prayers in the Slovenian language. But as I grew up, I learned to say them in English—the American language. I forgot them. But when I was back there, they said prayers in the Slovenian language, and I joined in. The words came back to me! As I heard the other people say them! You forget it, but then it came back.

In this country we loved to eat. Talk about eating!! My parents bought on the book. You know what I mean? Credit. Well, the furnace would run for two years, would be slow and shut down for two years. By the time my father had the book paid up to date, the furnace would shut down. We'd go back to living off the book.

To feed everyone, my father raised pigs and hogs; we had our garden; we had an immense garden. We worked in that. My mother was a field hand over in Europe. She knew how to hoe. She wore it down, she worked it down, from hoeing weeds. But we raised a lot of cabbage for sauerkraut. I often said, we lived on sauerkraut, potatoes and chitlings. That's what we lived on. In the winter we had our hams. Mother baked bread. My father would butcher these pigs. If you kept the hams too long, they would get maggots in the summertime. And we'd take them up to the cinder bank and bury them. But it got us through the winter.

But my father would have his beer with his food. I only saw my father drunk once, and he wouldn't come in the house that night. He must have been at a party or something. We had a grape arbor and he stayed out on this bench. He wouldn't come in the house the night because he was drunk. My mother was a good housekeeper and was strict about drink.

Mike Stefonich the beekeeper, Burd-Coleman, 1925.

But my father was a bit on the rough side, being an itinerant peddler over in the old country and getting married when he was nearly forty.

In the house we had this big iron stove in the kitchem. We heated it up and my mother would be kneading the dough, and put the pan in back of the stove so that the bread would rise, like magic you know. And then she would make these loaves. And, boy, that bread was the best thing, I thought. As a kid I ate that bread when it was good and warm. I can still remember it. She'd make doughnuts, fry them, and feed us kids. She'd feed us good. We had beans, baked beans, green beans, yes, bean soup. We lived off soups!

After we kids got big enough to appreciate Christmas, I remember not having much money. We didn't have much money. We never had much money. We would decorate our Christmas tree with toilet paper, and we would make little circles-like and make chains. And our Christmas tree would be decorated with these paper chains, with flour and water, with tinsel, and things like this. That was great. Then you got Christmas presents on Christmas day just like our children got them. We would get a Christmas tree here up on the hill above Burd-Coleman.

Q: When you were growing up, did your mom and dad expect you to act a certain way? Did they have certain rules for you?

We had to be in by dark. I can remember one night I didn't get home till after dark, and my father didn't come down the road for me. He went up through the woods. There were woods up above us. He came through the woods and I saw him going. He had a switch, and I scooted up and got home and got to bed before he did. He didn't want to beat me. He just wanted me to know if I didn't get home what the consequences were. Oh yes! I'll never forget.

But I grew up too fast. We had a neighbor that was somewhat younger than my father was. My father was, like I said, forty when he got married. And one day I went up to this man, a neighbor, and he and I had an argument. And I said, "If you don't pony up or do something right, I'm going to tell my father on you." He said, "You go and tell your father and I'll lick him and you both." It was a surprise to me. My father was strong. And up till that time I thought nobody could lick my father.

My father died—that was after Reading. I was going to Peirce Business School down in Philadelphia. I was the oldest of nine children and when my father died, I returned home. We still lived up in one of the company houses in Burd-Coleman. The family couldn't manage it, so I gave up my schooling. I was planning on being a Certified Public Accountant, which I never got to be. Anyway, I went to see Mr. Peterson and he felt that I was the type of person he wanted working. So I went to get signed up. The chief clerk, who later became my boss, said, "Nope, we're not hiring." He went over to the general manager, and I wasn't hired. I came home disgusted and told my brother. My brother went to this Peiffer Leibig and told him what happened. He talked to Peterson and Peterson sent word with my brother to come see him again. He gave me a card and *I got my job*. In spite of the chief clerk I got my job. I worked as a laborer for months.

In the meantime, they were having problems in the office. And they were having problems with the fellow timekeeping. He finally decided he was going to become a miner and work underground, which paid better. They had opened up an underground mine at No. 3. And he got a job there and they needed somebody for timekeeper. So, of course, Mr. Peterson shoved me in there. [Laughs.] Then this fellow who didn't want me to have a job was my boss.

Mrs. Warner Franklin

Warner came off the farm in Virginia and came up here and was working in the open pit in 1916. They ran jackhammers. Then you remember the first mine was opened over there at Burd-Coleman? This was No. 3 up there. He and John Zek were among the first that went in the underground mine. They all were afraid to go down there. They had worked in the open pit. You know a lot of people don't like it in the mines. They associated it all with coal, which is more dangerous. In the ore mine you don't have the gases and stuff; [instead you have] rockfalls.

At that time there were a good many black people living in our neighborhood. When they opened the underground mines they brought a lot of black people up. When they saw how it looked underground, they went back from where they came from; they wouldn't go underground. See, the company sent and got them during World War I, I guess. When they opened No. 3 mine in 1921 they left. The foreign-born volunteered. The blacks didn't want to go underground. They're like you, they don't like it underground. I don't like to go down in the basement. I feel hemmed in.

The underground made good money, though. The timbermen in the mines made the highest money; that's why Warner got to be a timberman. Of course, he knew a lot about carpentering because his father was a carpenter. He wedged up places where the men got to go under. He put in big timbers in there to hold that rock up and keep it from falling. As soon as they would blast, he would timber it up. And they would keep on blasting and go back in there till they got through there.

In the open pit Warner did blasting. I think at that time it was with

Packing powder for charges—blasting in the open pit, 1920s.

John Zek, who is dead. That was Tony Zek's father, who has this restaurant up here. And with Jack Jordan. There were two or three older men, too. They were buddies and worked together. Then sometime he worked with Paul Karinch. You heard of Joe Karinch? Well, my husband taught him how to work in the underground mines. Joe told me he would have got killed when he first went to work in the mines if it hadn't been my husband taught him everything he knew. Every time I see Joe at church, he always runs and hugs me.

They imported people in here by the trainloads during World War I. There used to be this man living over in North Cornwall who used to go down to North Carolina often. Even though they weren't allowed to recruit—he did it. It was against the law. They were short all over here.

He'd go down and bring them up—his relatives and all. His name was Mitchell.

So when we first came here in 1916 we rented this house for $3 a month. Bethlehem didn't own it. At first Lackawanna had it. We didn't have water in the house at first. We had pumps all up and down a row. There was a pump between these two houses, and then a pump at the corner, and a pump down at the other corner. And then, finally, they put water in the houses and then bathrooms in the houses. We had outside houses before that. Bethlehem Steel men would come around and turn them outhouses over. You see, there were big pits under them. They weren't sitting down on the ground like some of them. Then they had some kind of big old hose to clean them out. And finally they come around and put the porches on, with stoops. And they come around again. There was two rooms out back. They turned it into one big room—a big kitchen and a breakfast nook. There used to be a fireplace back there, chimney back there. In '52 they came around and remodeled it again. They come around and put all new floors in these houses, papered them and everything, and charged us $26 a month. And finally they decided to sell it. See, Bethlehem owned everything around here at that time. They decided to sell to the people living in them. If they wanted to buy them, they had first choice. We bought this house for $4,200.

When we first come here you could pick any house you want. There weren't that many people here yet. I mean just the open pits were going. Me and Warner picked this house because it had trees and a grape arbor in back. We had an apple tree back there and the wind blew it down. This house was empty. A whole lot of houses were empty all up and down. You could have your pick.

We didn't come here to stay. When I first left home, my father wanted me to come back. I was supposed to have the house, come back and build on and stay there. And that's what we came up here for—make money and go back to build onto the house. And after we got here my mother died. I think my oldest son was just nine months old when my mother died. And then I didn't want to go back. And finally my father lived up the street three years after that.

I didn't like it here for nothing. I used to say, "If I die, I don't want to be buried here." It was so much different from my place. Everybody had farms and was generally more friendly there. They tried to pick up churches and things to go to. And this little black church we had over here was nothing to me. Anybody could come in and preach there. Down home anybody couldn't go in your pulpit. You would have to have credentials to get in the church down there.

41

There were some old black families in Burd-Coleman when we came. Like the Scotts that's been there years and years. They were much older than I was, see. They were old when I came here. You see they had been here for years and years. And the kids were born here. They had children born here just like my children were born here. The Brisbanes have been here for a long time. One of them was kind of overseer over the furnaces in North Cornwall when they had that pig-iron stuff. He was a great-big man and he came from the South to Miner's Village a long time ago. They all drifted down to this place. And they stayed. They are all dead now.

Russell "Red" McDaniels

I was born in Lebanon, Pennsylvania, January 17, 1921. My father come from the coal regions up around Wilkes-Barre. He was a coal miner. He worked in the Shickshinny area. I do recall that he used to say how he drove mules in the mines. In other words, he was a mule driver at sixteen and hauled out the coal. Later he was a miner.

His sisters and his mother moved to Lancaster, Pennsylvania, and that's where he met my mother—in Lancaster. And then in early 1915 or 1916 he moved to Lebanon, Pennsylvania. And he was a crane operator in the Lebanon, Pennsylvania, area and he worked for Kaplan Brothers, scrap-iron manufacturers. They had a recycling plant.

A friend of his in Lebanon told him that they needed crane operators over here and that's how he got to Lebanon. He moved; he had no family at that time when he moved here. All my brothers and sisters were born in Lebanon, Pennsylvania.

He always said one thing: "I hope when my boys grow up they never have to work in the mines." That's what he said. He'd seen too many get buried in the coal mines—young fellows getting buried. Needless to say, if my dad would be living today I don't think I would've worked in the mines because that was against his wishes. My dad died during the service [World War II] and then when I came out of the service, that's when I went to the mines.

I was born and raised in the Twelfth Street area, the Twelfth and Church Street area. That's more dominated by Slovaks and Polacks. I was the only Irishman in that neighborhood. The living part of it was rough. Most of them had their own gardens. For firewood you went out to the old concentrator plant, where they dug up ties, and that's what you used for firewood. The coal—when you got the opportunity and a freight train stopped for water at the old pump station in West Lebanon—that's when you got your sons out there quick to take a couple

42

shovels full of coal off the train. That was our survival kit right there. I jumped up and threw the coal off; and then when the train moves out, then you bring your wagon over and load it up. We all did that in that neighborhood—mostly everyone did that.

We had a garden right across the street from the concentrator plant where the Coca Cola plant is right now. It was all gardens out where the office of the Coca Cola plant is, out on Sixteenth and Leamon. And who had them mostly was the people in our neighborhood. You could walk out there; it was only a half a mile and most of us in that whole neighborhood would have gardens out there. We grew mostly potatoes, carrots and tomatoes, and, of course, spring onions. We grew mostly potatoes for the winter, and cabbage. We grew sauerkraut and put it in barrels. Well, my dad never did that but my neighbors who were Slovaks did; they used to do it and give us some. We'd give them the cabbage and they would prepare it for us.

Later on, after I was born and raised on Twelfth Street—when I was eleven years old—we moved down to a section called Freeman Street. That's exactly right in front of the concentrator plant; it's the last street before you get to Sixteenth Street. It was never called Fifteenth. Fourteenth is behind and Sixteenth is up front but it was never called Fifteenth; it was called Freeman Street. It was a row of homes—about sixteen homes. And I lived in one of those homes there in my early age. You talk about the dirt from the concentrator! You couldn't sweep it off. You had to shovel the dirt off the pavement; that's how black it was. And it all depended on the way the winds were blowing. If it was going towards your home, you had to put paper in your window sills so the dirt wouldn't come in your bedroom or any other room. You had to put newspapers around there because if the wind was blowing in and they were melting their stuff, it would come right under your window. It was real thick and dusty as heck. I stayed here until I went in the service. Then I came home, then I got married, and I moved away from Freeman's Street. I have been here since then. That dirt would get in your throat and you would cough up awful black stuff.

There were complaints out. In fact, in them days that dirt was that bad that the women went to City Hall and complained about when they can't hang their wash out because it gets too dirty. So the company shut down on Mondays so the women could wash their clothes and hang them out. Instead of cleaning it up, they just shut down. Monday was washday for every woman in that neighborhood, because the dirt was that bad. But it didn't help you to wash. It went year round, too.

Lots of the men in that neighborhood were employed at the concy [slang for the concentrator] in the thirties. In fact, my three brothers are retired from the concy. One was an electrician and one worked in the chemistry and the other one was a mechanic. They all had good jobs, top-of-the-heap kind of jobs. I rub it in today yet, too, "I'm the only one that had to work for a living."

That neighborhood was a mix. There was very few Dutch in that neighborhood I would say. Out of a three-block area, Thirteenth, Fourteenth, Fifteenth, Freeman, I'd say there was only about three families that might've been Dutch. The rest were Slovaks and Czechs and Polacks; and one group of Irishmen down there. There was always good unity amongst the people—always! We had quite a few colored people worked at that and lived in the neighborhood.

Most colored people came from over the tracks, though, which is on the other side of the railroad tracks at Fourteenth Street. Over there in that neighborhood of Fourteenth Street, I'd say there was around ten colored families; and about four or five of those colored families worked at the concentrator. Most of them migrated from the South, but they were there before I moved in that area.

But when I was about twelve or thirteen years old, I would sit on the steps in that neighborhood. The concy whistle would blow and the men would come out. An old colored guy would come by and if he had a candy bar in his lunch bucket he'd give it to me. That's how I remember those colored people coming by—walking to work, mostly, in those days. A colored fellow by the name of Ike was one of them. I don't know his last name anymore. I think it was Green—Ike Green. I'm not sure, but he was a nice little colored gentleman and he worked at the concy for years. In fact, I think he died before World War II. I remember I still lived there yet and I didn't see him for a year. Evidently he died right before World War II, or either while I was in the service.

Our area, our neighborhood, was called the poorer section. That's what it was more noted for in that neighborhood where I was. They weren't the educated, but most of them did go through school though. But they were the poorer section or group in that neighborhood all the way from Twelfth Street down to Sixteenth.

When I came back from the service in 1945 and was still at Freeman Street, I got a job at the mines. Two other fellows in town which were working here—the three of us came out here from what we called "Hunky" town, where I lived. In fact, two of them were Slovaks, and me. We all got a job. The one never showed up and the other retired from here now. It was me and Frankie Steller and Janice.

We went right over here to this building across the street from the Cornwall Furnace. That was the office. That's where Joe Barnhart's office was. He was the big boss. We came in there and said, "Are you doing any hiring today?'' ''Yeah.'' You always had to have a reference from somebody from the mines. So who did I have a reference from but from another good Hunky: ''Frank Mahlic sent me out here and told me what to do.'' That's how we got a job. We talked with Joe Barnhart himself. And Mahlic was a timberman and he was pretty well liked. He was a good timberman, let's put it that way. He knew his job.

Matthew "Tip" Karinch

My parents came here in 1910 from Bellefonte. Before that they were in Yugoslavia. I was two month old, so I was born in September. They probably came here to Cornwall either November or December of 1910. My father had an uncle that was here. He went under the name of Martin Shoup as near as I recollect. I don't know if that was his right name or not, but a lot of times individual teachers or something changed the names to what they could pronounce. A lot of the kids didn't know English. They were brought up with parents that taught them the different languages and by the time they went to school they had a certain amount of English. But their names when they went to school were shortened by the teacher. Most of the foreign names were shortened.

Anyway, he was here. Well, he evidently wrote to my parents and told them to come. I think that's the way he—my great uncle—came over. Do you understand? Usually somebody made some arrangements for you;

Burd-Coleman furnace, early 1900s.

so my father went directly to Bellefonte because I had an uncle—my mother's brother—in Bellefonte at that time. Now between the two uncles I believe they got my father to come over. I believe when he first went over to Bellefonte they had these lime quarries, the Warner Lime Quarries. It was some lime company and I think they were mining the lime over there.

I don't know how my uncle found out about the furnaces over here, but they knew about them and my father came over here and he worked on three different blast furnaces. That was North Cornwall, Burd-Coleman, and the one in at North Lebanon. At that time Bethlehem didn't own any of them. Not the Cornwall furnaces. Most of those were affiliated with the Freemans who then had interest with the Colemans in those years back. They passed it down. As I said, he worked at North Cornwall, Burd-Coleman and North Lebanon. One would shut down and then they would go to another furnace. When this last one shut down here—I think this one was North Cornwall or Burd-Coleman, that shut down—then they went to the mines. Then he went underground; then he helped to start the underground mines.

We lived in Anthracite first [known locally as Goosetown]. We lived in a frame house first and that had a great-big yard with a garden. But, then, when Bethlehem Steel took over, there were three of those frame houses and they demolished the three. When we moved out we moved into the brick house across the street. In Anthracite there is a brick row; we moved into one of those houses. The next one we moved to near the ball diamond was the frame house. Eventually, I bought that house when Bethlehem Steel was selling homes. They owned practically every home around Miner's Village, too. They didn't in Rexmont. Most of those homes were owned by individuals. They owned the Brick Row going into Rexmont on the right-hand side—it used to be called "Grubbs Row." They were owned by the Bethlehem Steel going up towards the No. 4 mine.

There were a lot of bachelors that used to come in here to Goosetown at that time. Compared to the number of families that were around it was a lot, you know. Years ago whenever any immigrant came over here—if they sent for them—these people that were here housed them as boarders and kept them there while they were working. And as near as I know, it was mostly Yugoslavs and Italians; quite a few colored were here too. About half of the new people were colored at one time. There were the Johnsons, the Williamses, Derrings, Robinsons. They were there as long as anyone. Some of them were real old-timers; they were furnace men. A lot of them were carrying pig iron. They would get the pig iron out of the molds and stack it. A lot of them were great-big fellows. I don't remember having around there any Germans or any other nationality. This was really a string of pretty rough people where we were raised.

The housing was rough even by our standards. Usually you had about three bedrooms and a downstairs. Most of the time you had like an out-kitchen and a dining room and living room. And the toilets were outside. We didn't have no bathrooms inside. And your hot water you had on the stove. Each cook stove had an attachment there that you could take the lid off and dip the water out. And when you wanted to take a bath you had to get a bucket and dip out enough water. Everybody couldn't take water at the same time; you had to take turns on that. It worked like this: we started to get boiling water there and bathroom facilities, I believe right before the war, when Bethlehem Steel bought the place. When they took them over, then they started to put the water system in and that's when—in the late twenties when they were building Toytown—they run a water line down through there. So I imagine the water got into those homes sometime in the twenties. They didn't and they still don't have sewage. They have septic tanks and underground cesspools, and such things.

Then in Goosetown, everybody had pigs. When we were kids my father always had pigs, cows, chickens. Well, we had one of the bigger lots. That's why he continually moved until he got what he wanted, see. My dad always had enough vegetables and he knew how to preserve carrots and endive and celery and potatoes. Things like that were never bought; we raised all of that. When we were kids we picked wild strawberries, cherries, and then we had a lot of grapes. I remember he made his wine; he must've had about three or four big barrels of wine. He always had his wine in a milk bottle, in a quart like that. They would take turns you know. Whoever had the good wine—that's where the men would hang around until that was all and then they went to the next one. Sometimes they would get together on a holiday. Well, they didn't have too much time to socialize. See, they worked long and then the summer he had all his gardens. It was hot and they would go under the apple tree, and he made cider. We never wanted; my mother and father were good providers. We always had plenty to eat and clean clothes.

My mother could read; she used to decipher and write letters for most of the foreigners because she could read Croatian! But she could go ahead and read and translate these various letters that come here for people. A lot of them couldn't read and they were just a variation of Croatian. Yugoslavia at that time—where they come from was all under German rule at that point—was part of Austria-Hungary. But my mother used to write too; I remembered she was writing letters for everybody. She could go ahead and translate a lot of those German letters.

See, a lot of those Croatian words are the same as German. I would say that ninety-five percent of the people who came here couldn't read or write.

This was a great place for raising youngsters because you had all kinds of places to roam. Our biggest problem was we didn't have a swimming hole. You had one over here at the mines but that was so deep that they wouldn't leave you in. The kids would make dams and things like that.

If you got a licking in school and you came home and said something, you'd get another one—no questions asked. Or if somebody, one of the other kids, would come home and say so and so got a licking in school, "He did?" "Yeah." "What did he do?" "Well, he got the licking for it." As soon as you got home you got another one. My mother would have that switch right up above the stove—willow switches—thin ones. Boy, your behind and legs! My father never touched none of us. My mother did all the disciplinary action. My father never laid a finger on none of us.

I believe most of the foreigners, the mother took care of the kids. But the fathers would defend us if a bigger kid was fighting with the kids. Or if the father of another kid would push your kid around your father was quick to go down then and intercede and want to straighten things out. Then it was different; but as long as the kids were the same size, fighting, nobody bothered them. Because you see at that time you had brothers; so if two brothers licked one kid, the next time you caught one, then me and my brothers would go ahead and pounce on him. And that's the way this thing used to work out pretty good. It balanced itself out you know. Nobody really got hurt that bad; they were all friends about a couple days later. It was a very interesting neighborhood.

I was always busy. I was always doing things; you know when you're growing up. I was in Boy Scouts and sports and studies. So I was really busy from the time I was a teenager up until I got out of college and I got into the hotel.

Later on I decided to go to Lebanon High. Some of the fellows I met from Lebanon talked me into wanting to come to Lebanon High, because they were going to have track the next year. And that's another reason why I wanted to go to Lebanon High—for the track team. So my parents said I had to pay to go in. I had to pay tuition, so much a month to go. I know that later on the principal of Cornwall came to my house and they were just begging me to stay at Cornwall. I said, "No, I'm going to Lebanon." And I had some difficult times for a while, because they didn't have many foreign kids in Lebanon at that time. All the foreigners were out in the county in Cornwall and places like that. I had some problems with some of the boys but it worked out. When track season came around I made the track team. Then the next year I went out for football [in college] and I made the football team. I was in the Penn Relays. I did good; I think I was the only one that got a letter for track for running in the sprints. You had to win a first place. I ran against Harrisburg teams—John Harris, William Penn, Steelton, Lancaster, and Reading, where we had the big meet.

To go to track practice, I had to walk. Now from Sixth to Chestnut, where I went to school, we would go out to the fairgrounds. It's out near Sixteenth Street. We had to walk out and then we had to walk back after practice. Then I would walk all the way to Goosetown. That's a good distance. That's about eight or ten miles. I would jog most of the way. It didn't take me too long. The worst was during football season when it got dark. See, we practiced in September and October after school here at Third and Green. By the time you took your shower and everything else, there was no way for me to get home. I would always start walking and if anybody would pick me up, alright, or if they didn't, alright. That was not too hard—walking. I could make better time on the highway. You took a chance of now and then, of getting a ride. But cars were few. You know in 1928 and '29 there wasn't too many cars running around like now.

Well, I went to Lebanon [Valley] College. Boy, if I knew what was in store for me. I had a scholarship for tuition to play football, and I had never seen a football game. I played end in the backfield. I went out for practice with them. In fact, when I went out they didn't even give me a suit. First of all, I don't know whose shoes I got but they must've been that big [gesturing]. I had overalls and a sweatshirt. It wasn't long before they gave me a suit then. I told them. And I played every game. I started the first one and played every game. I worked very hard and I was pretty rough and that's why I started every one. I was fast and I could move around the same way [as] on the track. I used to run the half mile in two minutes, twenty seconds. The half mile is where I excelled. We played good teams. We played Penn State, we played Fordham, Brown, Villanova, Albright, Mount St. Mary's. We only had twenty-two players. I must have been the number twenty-two because I was the smallest guy on the squad. I only weighed 145 pounds at that time. Though I played end most of the time, they would put me any place they needed somebody to take a bump or two.

When I went to Lebanon Valley there were only three Catholics up there; they didn't mix too well. I really got along the best with the people that taught Bible. But there was some of those people that was nasty to the Catholics. You wouldn't believe it. I had to have everything perfect before I would get a proper grade, just enough to keep carrying me over.

Peter Rossini, Sr., and family, early 1920s.

Things were tough because they wanted you to take some extra courses. See, you had to pay two bucks for some of those extra-exam courses. They knew I was one of those guys who was always trying to get ahead.

Peter Rossini, Jr.

I was six years old when we come down in the early 1920s. We came down in an old 1917 Dodge touring car. My dad had a couple of spare tires in the back of the touring car and you had those fender-expansion things for each fender to hold somebody's luggage. In this touring car there were four kids piled in the back, Mom and Pop plus some of the luggage, you know. We got all the way down to Hummelstown—they were just making this bridge there in Hummelstown—and the state cop stopped us and Pop had to dig down through all this stuff and find the title to the damn car. When you saw an out-of-state license then, they thought about stealing. It's not like you see now with all the different states. But he had to dig down for the damn title. It took us eleven and a half days. I think we stopped at some hotels. It was just Pop doing the driving. You come down on what they called the Lincoln Highway; the telephone poles were painted blue and yellow. Route 30, that's the Lincoln Highway, as they called it. So that's what you followed all the way down through here, and sometimes you would get lost.

I think Peterson, the General Manager-to-be, and Pop came down together first before we came. I guess they were looking over where they were to be starting the mines. They had made contact with Bethlehem Steel. See, Pop worked at different mines up there in Minnesota's Mesabi Range. He came here because the mines up there weren't too active in the wintertime, especially the open mine because of the cold weather and on account of shipping ore. There wasn't too much work there in the winter. He was wanted because he was in the underground up there as a foreman.

I was born in the Range. My one brother was born in Baudette and two were born in Crosby. Dad, before he first bought that Dodge, used to use a bicycle to go back and forth to work. But when he bought that Dodge, he drove that home, without learning how to drive or nothing. He came down the road and you better look out!

Dad got my godfather a job over here in Cornwall when he came. He came down from the Range and he was working here with us. Some of them came from Wisconsin. But when they first came, they came down in 1924. He had gone to the station, down at the Cornwall station here, to pick him and his wife up. And they got their home down here then.

Nobody in Cornwall knew anything about underground mining until

51

my dad and them came down from the Range. Dad was the one that showed them how to use a blasting pole in the mines. Nobody knowed about them. See, when they made these fingers to go up in the ore body, well, the ore would hang up. So what they did was to tie powder around them on the pullies, go to the mountains, cut a bunch of poles, maybe tie a couple together, and shove them up there with long Q's and then blowed it loose.

For the open pit they brought a bunch of Mexicans up here one time. They run a passenger train up here and they unloaded them at the end of where the railroad tracks are. They had a boarding house on the one side over here in Miner's Village. It was this last house up over the hill; down in the back part they had a bunch of shacks. The shacks were about half as big as a regular miner's house. The place was like a barracks where they would sleep, and the other place was a kitchen and everything. I don't know if they brought them up for cheap labor or what, but there were a few Mexicans here. But then later on, some of the Mexicans left, but some of them stayed around here.

Many for the underground came from Wisconsin and Minnesota and maybe Michigan too. I think some came from the open pit and then went underground, too. I guess the pay was probably better then.

When we first came Mom was looking for a house in one of the villages here, see. Well, they showed her some at Miner's Village, but she didn't care much for them houses over there. Then she got this house up here in Burd-Coleman, second [to] last door on the left. So we was living there until 1924, and then we moved here to our present place in Burd-Coleman. I mean she wanted a house without the hill behind it, so the guy in it moved out of here. We moved down here.

There weren't many Italians around here. That was hard because we usually visited the Italians' families because we spoke Italian. Most of the neighbors were Dutch around here; there were a lot of Dietzes because old Charley Dietz lived up here. His sons Jack and Joe and the Beards were related. Oh, Martinis used to live up at the end house up over the hill—they were Italian. Over at Miner's Village there were more—the Metleys. Rexmont and Robesonia had more too.

We were pretty independent and self-sufficient. Mom was a good worker; she could do anything. She learned to sew up in Minnesota. She bought a Singer sewing machine when she come down here. She made dresses at that time and I think she got a $1.35 or something for a dress from Harkins. She could just pick everything up on her own. She used to fix our shoes—put leather on them and everything. She made all our clothes. When you bought flour or sugar you got them cotton bags. You could make underwear or aprons out of it or pillowcases. She used to knit or crochet our stockings and our sweaters. I wore knickers and long stockings. I still have a lot of stuff that she has made.

We always had a garden. Mom used to can a lot of stuff, like beans. I'll tell you what—we went out all day up there picking huckleberries in the brush. We even got lost up there in the hills above Burd-Coleman. Well, we'd come back with water buckets full of berries—the whole gang. We went up toward Mount Gretna road. But, see, recently the timber growed up. There was no light for the huckleberries then.

The boys would go up over the Second Mountain to get wood. Bethlehem Steel left you cut the trees down up there. So you would cut down whatever wood you needed. They used to split them up there in about ten-foot length so you could handle them. When we got them down here we got a sawbuck. You sawed it by hand and usually sawed with two guys, one on each end—push and pull back and forth. Then we'd fill the wood box up.

See, all this stuff is important because we didn't have to buy a thing. Well, you had everything from your garden; you had your tomatoes that you made tomato sauce with for spaghetti, and tomato paste. You didn't buy any of that, you made your own. Celery and lettuce run into late November and December; the celery and stuff you would bury under some boards in the garden and it would keep like a root cellar.

I want to tell you, all these foreigners, especially the Italians, made good wine. My dad made wine with good California grapes—thirty-six cases at a time. You would make it for the whole year. You can't buy good wine like that now. You just made it from juice without sugar; then what you drained out of there was the second wine you made to which you added water and sugar and then that fermented. That was an everyday wine; you'd drink it instead of water. But the good wine was for special occasions. But whenever we would get a cold, Dad or Mom would cook this wine up and heated it up for us. They put nutmeg in. They'd get it good and hot and you drank it down and you sweated with it. It was a good cold remedy.

With the family being so close, the brothers stuck together. We might've picked on each other but let any outsider come in, boy we stuck together. I know a lot of families of brothers here; they would argue and fight but let some outsider come in and they all stuck together and the outside guy was in trouble. We were only afraid of Carpenter's kids from Rexmont.

THE ENGINEERS

Mrs. P. L. Steffensen

We came to Lebanon in the spring of 1934 to stay three months, as there was a temporary job for my husband at the concentrator, and then to be transferred to Bethlehem. We lived in a small, makeshift, light-housekeeping apartment in Lebanon. After a year it became evident that my husband was not going to be transferred to Bethlehem, as he was doing a good job improving the operations of the different processes at the "concy" and making it more productive than ever before. So we applied for one of the vacant houses in Toytown, Cornwall Borough, because most of the people in management lived here. We moved to Cornwall in the spring of 1935 and are still here in the same house, except that through the years the house has been remodeled several times to suit the needs of our growing family and our social activities.

At first there was such a small group of engineers and their wives that when we invited them for bridge there were just enough people for two tables. Eventually the group grew in numbers.

For the first few years I did not bother to learn to drive as my husband took the car to work and, what's more, it was next to impossible to get baby sitters in the daytime. The women who wanted to earn extra money worked in the dress factories in Rexmont, Quentin and Lebanon. But we did go out in the evenings, as we could get high-school girls to baby-sit. In Cornwall Center there was only a post office, general store with two gasoline pumps, and a butcher shop. We could order our groceries in the mornings and have them delivered in the afternoons. Milk and baked goods were delivered three times a week. We still have milk deliveries, but all the other services are gone. For all our other needs we had to go to Lebanon.

Most of the engineers and their wives were from out of state, so we had no relatives to fall back on. Most of us were young and lonely, so we would get together in the afternoons and play bridge; we had to take our children with us. When pleasure-driving was introduced during the Second World War, we felt even more isolated and depended even more on one another for recreation. The women would play bridge in the evenings as well, while the husbands baby-sat and, then, the men would get together to play poker and we would stay home with the children. To brighten up Saturdays we would have "progressive dinners"—it gave us an excuse to wear evening clothes, for which we had no other use during the war years. The men, of course, could not be persuaded to wear a tux.

Just before the outbreak of World War II we got a second car: a brand new Ford coupé, with all the frills, for $750! Sounds like a fairy tale, doesn't it? I felt liberated even though with gas rationing, I could make only one trip a week to Lebanon (I did not drive the Ford, I got stuck with the gas guzzler).

After the war was over, life was normalized and we were able to resume our own individual lives. Bethlehem Steel had enlarged its facilities and there were more engineers living in Cornwall and Lebanon. We were also able to make friends in Lebanon and the surrounding areas.

Once the "concy" was running at full production, my husband turned his attention to research. A pilot plant was built. One of the projects was the development of a process for pelletizing of low-grade iron ore for large-scale commercial use; up to that time the process did not get past the laboratory stage. Eventually the process, with some variations, was adopted throughout the world. The pellet plant in Cornwall was one of many designed by my husband. There were other equally challenging projects, so a Raw Materials Research Laboratory was built "on the hill" in Lebanon. My husband was the manager.

Even though Cornwall never looked like a typical mining town, in the days when Bethlehem Steel owned most of the property it was a company town. The general manager's wife was deeply involved in the life of the community. During the Great Depression used clothing was collected and everyone who cared to contribute her time was encouraged to meet in the home economics room in the old schoolhouse to help mend it. A well-baby clinic was held once a month. Volunteers were needed for that.

We had a pleasant social life after the war. Maybe we would just ask friends over and sit on the patio, or we would have a buffet supper. There was a family living right in Toytown who had twelve children—eight of them girls. Some of them were my baby sitters for many years. They would also help with the dishes and the serving when we had parties. We had many buffet parties then.

Once a year we had a steak party for the men at the Raw Materials Research Laboratory, usually in September when everybody had had their vacations. The engineers were a nice group and we were very informal. They said they wanted Rita's scalloped potatoes and her tossed salad. So all day long I would prepare the food. There were about twenty of them and they were all young, so they had very good appetites. I would have two big dishes of scalloped potatoes and a huge bowl of tossed salad, and lots of coffee. They always had a good time. There were frequent outbursts of hearty laughter that I could hear upstairs. I told my husband, "Don't you every make any remarks about the women playing bridge and cackling and making noise, because when your gang laughs it shakes the whole house."

As befits a small company town, a pecking order was observed by the female members of the management community presided over by the general manager's wife. I knew where I stood, but it was a delicate balancing act, not one hundred per successful. She was generous, friendly, outgoing and helpful—perhaps too helpful. That caused resentment and friction, as not everyone could take criticism and suggestions on how one should conduct oneself. It is hard enough to cope with one's own family, let alone a whole group with their individual personalities, backgrounds, and levels of education. It was a frustrating and fruitless task, hard on everybody. But that was a long time ago.

Some of the engineers lived where Karinchville is now. It used to be called North Cornwall. The general manager lived in a mansion that was torn down later, but which then faced the open pit. Nearby was a smaller house with a bell tower built of the same type of stone. You'd never know that they had existed. There is another house made of sandstone near the entrance to the Methodist Church Home. Dr. Schaffer lives there now. One of the engineers had lived there. We could've lived in any one of those houses, but we just preferred to be here because it was centrally located, close to the school, and close to the general store. By that time we had remodeled the house in such a way that it suited our needs.

The workers lived in Miner's Village, Burd-Coleman, Goosetown and Paradise. When we first came here they told us that the homes were seventy-five years old. We have been here since '35. I'd say they are now over a hundred years old, actually a hundred twenty-five years old. But they are solidly built. And after the war Bethlehem Steel really made a lot of improvements in them. At first they had no bathrooms and they had no heat upstairs, so they fixed them up so they would have heat upstairs and indoor bathrooms. The rooms are still tiny even though the houses look so big. But they are durable and their walls are thick.

Until recently we had no street signs and no numbers in Cornwall. Even now people want to know "what street are you living on?" I know it's Pine. But try to ask me to give you directions to other streets and I wouldn't be sure. We don't say Maple Street or Juniper Street; we say where so-and-so used to live. We have our own landmarks. We don't pay any attention to the names of the streets here.

Bethlehem Steel ceased operations and sold its property. Most of the engineers are gone. Cornwall is just a lovely little town with no downtown and no billboards. Cornwall has been home to us for fifty years.

Community

"*Community*" *is always filled with personal meaning. Observers and residents of Cornwall have different interpretations of what did and did not make a community and what led to the decline of a spirit of "neighborliness," "togetherness" and community.*

Robert Arnold, Sr., best describes the forces which compelled each small village to go its own way. To him and most others, survival initially meant separation; one had to cooperate primarily with others in one's own small village to secure the basics of life. In a village setting, extreme separation and provincialism became virtues; outsiders were suspect and unwelcome.

Other forces worked toward cohesion and a sense of community. Mrs. Franklin relates how the stores in the borough meant much to people; they sponsored community events and sent peddlers to remote areas of the borough. Matthew Karinch relates a fascinating story of how he used the Blue Bird Inn as a base of good will for all borough people—workers as well as managers, coal "crackers" as well as the foreign-born. Building on that foundation, "Tip" financed a strong "semi-pro" baseball team—the Cornwall Athletic Club. Community spirit was enhanced; nearly all in the borough attended games and took pride in the team's accomplishments. Who could not identify "Snowball" Clapper, or not recite the team's unblemished records before the advent of television? After World War II, it was natural that the public-spirited Karinch would finance and build the new housing developments in Karinchville and Toytown.

Mrs. Warner Franklin

I remember Bill Hawkins used to have a store and butcher shop down here. They sponsored the Black Sox, the black ball team in Cornwall. It was just like having some reason to get people to go into town. I don't think they got anything. If they did, it wasn't very much. We didn't pay anything to go up there and see it. Just an outlet for something to do. And they used to play the band. They sent their band out to play, to charge people, so I don't know how much money they was making. But I don't remember paying nothing. They had stands to sell something. They made it that way. You know, sell hot dogs and ice cream and stuff like that.

He had the butcher shop, see. It was just like a company store. You buy down there and pay—at first when Lackawanna owned it. And you could get credit when Hawkins had it [later]. All the stores were credit.

It was located in Cornwall Center. When you come into Cornwall you see a big-old building right up from the post office with a lot of flowers planted around. That used to be our post office, and the butcher shop and stuff. But now the post office and the bank went together. That was originally a railroad station, where the bank and post office is now. That's where the train used to stop. That's where Hawkins was.

They had everything. They had ice in there. The best liver you could buy was when you bought that fresh liver, and they sliced it off for you. It wasn't old frozen liver like you buy in stores now. Dutch people used to have it before Hawkins. They even baked bread. You could smell that bread all over Goosetown, almost. They came around with this bread and cookies, and anything else. You could buy anything in that store, but an automobile.

Robert Arnold, Sr.

The communities first were apart since it took so much to survive. Miner's Village had a little spring that came out of the mountain, and then people would go there in the evening with their buckets to get water for their hogs and get water for their houses. For washing, Rexmont was the same; Burd-Coleman was the same. See, there were springs in the mountain and they had an iron pipe dug in and caught one of these springs. Then it came out in this pipe; then they could hold their bucket under this pipe and then they carried their water home. And then later on when Bethlehem Steel built these homes in Toytown, why then they formed a water company. Later they turned it over to the borough, when they started in collecting dues.

Building Pine Street in Toytown, 1927.

Toytown was all built beforehand and put together. These homes were built in 1926 by the Minder Home Corporation of West Virginia. They put each home in a rail car—the whole home—and all they had to do was mark each one and put them together like a jigsaw puzzle. And they were all Bethlehem Steel laborers that put these homes together, except the person who hung the doors and put the windows in; he was with the Minder Home Corporation in West Virginia. They shipped them from down there, one car, one home, and they dug the cellars with scoops and horses. They didn't have any backhoe or anything then. Then they put the wall in and then they put the floor in. Then one day a whole gang from the Minder Home Corporation from Huntington, West Virginia, came up and they put the twenty-five homes up in one day—the frames. All around they were twenty-four feet square and twenty feet high, and then they put all this up. Then the carpenters and stuff put the rest on and the roof on. One contractor had the roof, the other fellow had the contract for the furnaces, and another contractor was a bricklayer and he put in the fireplaces. But outside of that the rest of the stuff was all built by the Bethlehem Steel then. They built twenty-five homes and they appropriated $60,000; that was a little more than $2,000 for each home. That's what they cost them. That included everything.

They pretty much look the same; one home is peaked, the next one is long and the next one is peaked, and the next is long. They weren't selling the homes at all; they rented them. People that worked in the Bethlehem Steel could live in them. Before this the Freemans owned all the homes here.

These homes cost eighteen dollars to rent and the Freeman homes cost five dollars to rent. But then every two years or so they went up. They were eighteen for four years and then they went up to twenty-six, then it went up to thirty-four and then it went up to forty-four. And then later after forty-four, Bethlehem Steel started going out of business. Then they sold the homes in 1957 to the people who lived in them. I was here in 1929, and lived here for fifty-two years. At first the company only rented about half of them.

There were things going on in each small community. Rexmont had a band of their own; Quentin had a band. Before the school bands came out, why every town had a band. And then when the schools started in, then the town bands were popular, about forty or fifty years ago. This was a little bit before the 1930s. In 1928 they formed a band right there at Cornwall. The first band was called the "Miners." They weren't professional like school bands now. If you could blow a horn or something you could play. Sometimes you'd hit a wrong note and it didn't make much difference. The horns were pretty expensive. I used to get a lot of horns then at the station because they came in C.O.D. I got horns that cost $175 for the Rexmont band. The people were community people. There were no regular musicians. In the beginning they didn't have any uniforms. They just had black pants and a white shirt. And they had miners' caps. See, they were miners out there with a miner cap on with a little light on in the front. That's the uniform they had.

But don't let this community stuff fool you. It could be dangerous. When they had a picnic or carnival in Rexmont, for example, they had a

Golden Eagle Band of Rexmont at Penryn Park, adjoining Mount Gretna, summer of 1927.

little booze stand back there. Then them fellows were half drunk and they'd shoot anybody, so I wouldn't go near there.

The firemen had a picnic one time in Rexmont and one fellow got that drunk that he'd hit anything, even if a tree was in front of him. They hit him and they had to put him away and laid him down there for a little while. When he couldn't walk they just laid him down for a little while. He would've broke his fist and everything because he was going to hit anything in front of him. They only had the picnic one time and about a dozen were drunk. Then in the evening when the picnic was over, they had this wheelbarrow, but they didn't have no rubber tires; they had steel tires. Then they would set the fellow up and push the wheelbarrow there. Then he set in the wheelbarrow and his legs would hang out over the front, and you could hear this wheel when they were hauling them home. They had enough booze there for a dozen fire companies.

Then each community had what they called a bully. Rexmont had two bullies, Bully Woody Carpenter and Bully Adams; and Schaefferstown had a bully; Mount Zion had a bully. And if Schaefferstown then came to Mount Zion and they knew they were from Schaefferstown, why they would start fighting right away. Not any reason, except that they were bullies. Miner's Village didn't have no bully, nor did Quentin. Rexmont was the only one. Burd-Coleman and North Cornwall didn't have one either.

There were great fights. Back at Mount Zion I know a lots of times they had fights. I never went there to the hotel, but I went to the picnic. When they had a picnic sometimes they'd come together. Now and then they had kerosene lamps, and one fellow would take a bottle against the lamp and out went the lamp. Then it was dark and they wouldn't know who they were hitting or anything. Chairs and everything would be broken to pieces.

Rexmont Hotel and Schaefferstown Hotel and Mount Zion Hotel were the three that I knew that had bullies that came together. And then over in Lancaster County they had two fellows there. They were big, husky; they were both over six feet tall and they weighed over two hundred pounds. Several local bullies went over to Lancaster County to buy a horse and they stopped off over there at the White Oak Hotel in Lancaster. They went in for a drink of beer and this local bully came up to the bar. Then, when he was trying to drink his beer, they bumped him around. These two were pretty good men, local men from here, so they bullied around. One of our local bullies cracked this Lancaster bully and had him up in the air. The boss, the hotel manager, came in and said, "Don't throw him down." They threw him down on the floor, and the manager told our people to get out and stay out. Sometimes the police

61

would pursue. At that time the State Police were on horses; they weren't on motorcycles or anything. Well, if a fellow had a good horse and buggy, he could outrun the State Police and they couldn't catch him.

Matt Karinch

Each little town in the borough was isolated and stayed together pretty well. See, they were pretty far apart. You didn't see any reason to walk to Burd-Coleman, unless you had some relation over there. You didn't go because when you were younger, you only took a chance at getting a beating. You didn't wander too far away from your own territory. But if you were up around fourteen or fifteen years old, you were taking a chance. Especially if you went by yourself, there was always two or three over there waiting for you. Now, if we saw a lone kid coming over from Burd-Coleman, walking over this way or something, then he got it, he didn't turn around and leave. It didn't matter if he was black, white or anything. It ain't no difference. We had boundary lines from Goosetown to Rexmont. There was a mock orange tree—that's where you stop. Even if his father worked with your father in the mines. That didn't make any difference. When they were kids they didn't wander down here, no way! The other fellows wouldn't allow another fellow from Rexmont to go with a girl from Goosetown. Huhmmm, he got clobbered. When I was a kid, I remember those bigger guys every once in a while would go back to Rexmont and have a free-for-all. Just the fellows from Goosetown that were sixteen or more. They would go back there because towards the end, Goosetown had the best scrappers. That's because there were more foreign boys in that area and they were rough. They used to hammer the hell out of the Carpenters back in Rexmont. See, that was pretty near a lot of Carpenters and Petrys and they were a different group from Rexmont. They weren't as good fighters. In other words, the people in Goosetown were mostly laborers and they were kind of used to roughness. I did my share of scrapping too.

The church unified us. We attended anything that they had at that time. My mother made us go—all of us. You went and before you left the house she'd check your ears and everything else. You didn't go to church or school dirty; you'd see that your hair was combed and clean clothes and before you go, "Did you wash?"

See, that church was so situated that Miner's Village had their way to get there and Burd-Coleman had their way, and we had our way. Sometimes I think it must've been planned to be placed where it was—at the boundary of the towns. Everybody got along good. Near as I know, down around there [the church] was no problem with anybody. It's just

Olde Golden Key Hotel, late 1800s, now Blue Bird Inn.

in the summertime the kids didn't have too much to do and it was so easy to fight. At that time you'd get a lump here and there and a few stones thrown at you.

My real contribution to Cornwall was the Blue Bird Inn. The owners couldn't make it go in 1935. These people that were in before couldn't make it work. Through sports and everything else, I thought that I wouldn't have too much of a problem. At that time you could buy a beer on credit. It was furnished and all I needed was one month's rent. Do you understand? And then I had enough business sense. I had studied business administration and I knew enough about agreements and things like that. I took an option to purchase the thing. At that time I took an option to purchase for what the bank had the mortgage on, which was $9,000. Well, I worked at it and I got a couple of hundred dollars from my mother for working capital; the beer—you could go ahead and get credit, and you would slowly be paying for it every week. I kept my nose right there to work and I had a good clientel and I worked hard at it and it was just a question of time.

The younger people and the people from the mines were starting to come over. Then I had a lot of people here from the coal regions; they were starting to come a little, in like '36 and '37, to organize the mines.

63

Unions were pretty strong at that time and I had a lot of that. Oh, a lot of them union fellows used to come over and gather here. But I wouldn't tolerate no union talk in there or anything else. You came in there to drink and I don't want to hear nothing about work. Many were opposed to the union. It was easy to get a scrap. But I could control it very good. I never had no fights there. If anybody wanted to fight, why I would ask them to go outside and then I would referee for them. They would go ahead and I had some dandies. All bare knuckles. If they had an argument inside the Blue Bird, then I threw them outside as soon as they got a little hot. "Look, I don't tolerate that! If you're going to settle this now, go out and have your fun. But I am going to referee to see that it's fair!" Sometimes I would promote it for a little action.

On Saturday morning those coal crackers used to come over there and they were always talking about how tough they were. I would edge them on, Joe Hale, Taebers, Rinkers, and most of them were interrelated, brother-in-laws and that. They lived in a big boarding house and they were always fighting in the middle of the street. But they had some good bare-knuckle fights. Then after one would win, they would go ahead and I'd clean up and come back and given them something to wash the blood off their faces. We had some real good brawls; they were always on the outside though. See, we had an enclosure where they park, for when they used to keep the wagons under. Then lots of times I would leave them go in there in a stall. I'd say, "Go over there in a stall and stay in that stall." There I could control it pretty good. After you once make them fight, you'd be surprised how you eliminate stuff. But I used to belt them quick as soon as somebody got out of hand. Well, I had the training for it you understand. I had the strength to handle it, so I didn't take no crap from nobody that came in—that's that.

The unions really liked us. They used to come over there—different groups—when they were having their grievances and all. I just wouldn't tolerate no arguments; ordinarily the two organizers would be there—the union men. Hyle used to be there—the representative for the Bethlehem Steel. I also believe Miller was from the union. "When Hyle's here I don't want to hear nothing about the union, or anybody getting started in a discussion. When Miller's in here I don't want to hear any of you non-union men starting nothing." If you hadn't done that I would've had a free-for-all there all the time. It would hurt my business. This way I got them both—they both came there. But I have to say, I was quite diplomatic on handling most situations and I knew how to talk them out of it, and I knew when force was necessary. And when force is necessary, you do it first; you don't wait for the other guy to hit you. So you got to do it first if you're going to throw somebody out. You see you have no

64

Cornwall Athletic Club at Goosetown, 1920s.

problems. You don't wait until he grabs you; you grab him first, especially when you're going to do something like that. And that was the secret on a lot of that stuff—knowing who to pacify and how you could straighten it out. You had to use diplomacy on one another.

This was a gathering place for everybody. When we had ballgames on Saturday afternoon, everybody would come over here. Then the place was so full you couldn't walk, couldn't get through the dining room, kitchen or anyplace. I had a bar, dining rooms, everything! And we lived on the second floor. See, in '35 I got married. Then we fixed up the one floor and the third floor.

I had that much business—I used to have to serve them on the second floor and then the porch—we had a big screened porch. We had parties like Saturday nights. See, at that time one guy had the car and he maybe brought two other couples or another couple when they were going out—whoever had the car. They would take turns on cars; everybody didn't have a car at that time.

I always liked baseball. We had part of a ball club in town before, but it wasn't too active. It was the Cornwall Athletic Association. That was the Athletic Club all the way back to 1911. In the twenties it was known as the Cornwall Athletics Association. Then around 1930-31, I was one of the officers with it. When I went in business in 1935, I bought them uniforms with "Blue Bird Inn" on them. Then, after we organized the A.C., then in 1938 we started to play. In 1939, we had the first semipro game. We played it here. We made the ball diamond in '38.

Before, the club played in Goosetown. Before that they played at Burd-Coleman. But before that they played at Goosetown because we had more players at Goosetown. They had moved it to Burd-Coleman around 1924. They played there until 1931. Then we moved it back to Goosetown. We played there until I built the diamond. Ever since we have been playing here.

We moved the field from Goosetown here to the Blue Bird. We did it for a number of reasons. First of all that was a swamp. And this was high and dry. You could play there. If I'm sponsoring the team—putting the money into the team—I want to get some benefit out of it for the hotel. So it worked two ways for me. I promoted it, organized it, got the uniforms, paid the bills. If they were short of money, I put the money in. In the Depression they didn't have uniforms. After I got in there I bought uniforms. In 1939 we got into a different league—semipro ball.

We had the pick of Lebanon County for good ball players. We heard about other good ball players by picking up the paper; there'd be a lot of leagues and you'd follow who had a good batting average, and who had the write-ups; and you would contact them. There were a lot of leagues at that time, especially up in Harrisburg. I had ball players from the Coal Regions, from Lancaster, from Harrisburg.

Before, they had old railroad leagues years back. You see, they played because they got good jobs. I think the railroad was paying them something extra. There were other teams in the late 1930s besides ours, Palmyra, Lebanon. That was pretty fast baseball. We got in the Old Lebanon Valley League, which was Palmyra, Cornwall, Manheim, New Holland, Newmanstown, Robesonia, Reading, Tremont and Pine Grove. Different sponsors helped, like Dr. Walters from Pine Grove took care of Pine Grove payroll; Tremont Coal Company took care of Tremont. They had the first lights around that area. When Myerstown got in the Goodwill Fire Company helped. They had slot machines so they could sponsor—[I mean with] money. Newmanstown had an athletic club with Frank Raeder. He picked up the big tab. At Manheim Bob Frey, who had the hotel, picked up the tab and looked for ball players. At Cornwall I took care of it. Certain businessmen that were interested in sports would do that; now nobody will do it. Everybody thinks they made a lot of money. That's what they were saying over here at the Athletic Club. I had built up a reserve for them for scholarships. I got tired of hearing that Tip's making all the money. So I said, "Alright, let someone else try it one year." So, they did. It went through three thousand dollars of Athletic Club money that I had set aside. They found out that it wasn't that rosy. Players cost; that was one of the last years we had it. We had players from Carlisle Barracks. They were just about big-leaguers.

We had some financial restrictions in bidding for their services. The only bidding was done locally on fellows like Snowball Clapper, a really good pitcher. He was a booze hound. I used to give him $50 a day, a lot

Palmyra vs. Cornwall, 1957, played in ball park built by Matthew Karinch at Cornwall.

of money in those days. And, then, everybody at the bar would take a donation for him. He was worth it. They used to pack in to see him.

We built the stands ourselves. I bought the lumber. The fellows all chipped in—different carpenters. The fellows I sold the first lots to in my development were carpenters. I gave them the lots for a hundred dollars apiece. So anything I asked them to do they did. They built the bleachers; in one we could seat a thousand. We filled them on Saturdays and Sundays when we played our games. Towards the end we won all the time.

Baseball just petered out in the middle of my housing development. I started it so my players would have some housing. They could help constructing them, too. That's how it started. The first buyers after that moved here in '42. These were neighbors. Marshall Keener was the first one that moved here in 1942. And Wilmer Ruhl; both could have been from Quentin. Well, anyway, the development really started about '46 or '47. My brother-in-law needed a house, my brother needed a house. I had a couple of other fellows that I had hired. From there on it took off. I built it in sections. I got the first land from Blanche Molley, who owned the Blue Bird before me.

It was all trial and error, you understand? I had people over here who called me crazy when I started. I couldn't sell them fast enough after I started. But first I had to bury a lot of big concrete pillars. I had to get a big shovel and dig big holes. And push them in. If you would have seen it. It was a dangerous situation the way it was. You had big rocks which kids could fall off of. Some of the concrete pillars were up fifteen to

Bird's-eye view of Karinchville shows old inn at the bottom, workers' cottages and new development.

twenty feet. And rock, and pipe!! If beforehand they wanted to give it to me, I wouldn't have taken it. Only when I started developing did I want it.

I financed practically all of the homes; I signed the notes. I would build them and sell them. Most of them were sold when the homes were completed. I did the building! Then we drew the agreement that I would build the house before I sold the land. Rod Grimes was the first one; the rest were built by me. If people's plans for houses suited me, I would built it. I wanted to blend the homes.

As I progressed I would extend the roads farther and farther. I supplied everybody with the water at one time. I had three wells. Per year it would cost them between seven and fourteen dollars. I also charged them electricity too. I've had no problems with my septic tanks. Very little sewage problems. In Goosetown you had a problem; you still have a problem. It seeps over to the creek. You could smell it. And the other from Burd-Coleman and the school used to seep over into that other creek. But up here it was O.K.

See, I didn't just try to sell the house for the buck. If they were the right kind of people I tried to help them. We still carry mortgages on the people. I look at it this way: maybe I wouldn't have had the sales with the good people. I made some and I lost some. I interviewed the people. And if I had trouble with people, I'd buy it back.

The Company

Bethlehem Steel dominated the social and economic life of Cornwall and Lebanon City. The degree and character of that domination was so total that outsiders were astonished when they saw the realities close up. Russell "Red" McDaniels' interview is important because it suggests how Bethlehem Steel kept potential competition out of the county and how the lower-paying jobs of the shirt factories were essential to support workers' families, especially when Bethlehem was closed.

Bethlehem Steel did provide a lot to Cornwall, however. John Yocklovich, in his interview, relates how the workers secured water for the borough. More important was the company's unstated policy of "loaning" equipment and supplies to workers who could not afford to pay for improvements on their homes or for construction supplies. Another practice was the hiring of family and friends. All these practices cemented the relationship between workers and company, and, as Mrs. Franklin relates, made it difficult later to organize a union in the borough.

Russell "Red" McDaniels

Right before World War II Bethlehem Steel was the dominating power here in Lebanon. If you were employed by Bethlehem Steel you were considered pretty good employment. There was very little around—a few shoe factories and a couple of dress factories and shirt factories—but they didn't pay what Bethlehem Steel did. But you must remember—be a little subtle—the people themselves didn't want another industry. Bethlehem dominated at one time.

Q: Why did they allow shirt factories and dress factories in then?

Lots of them were here before Bethlehem Steel was here. Most of those shirt factories and dress factories were dominated by the Kaplans, the Cantors, and Park Silk, which is Seigfield. Most of them came from New York. They came to this town here and set up factories.

Q: Whom did they employ?

Mostly women.

Q: Were they mostly the working laborers' wives?

Yeah. The women that had to help support the family.

Q: Did Bethlehem Steel and the shirt factories cooperate?

They had what they called management banquets, I remember. I don't think they do that no more. This was where the management of the shirt factory and the clothing factory and the Bethlehem Steel management would get together. They would have a banquet. They called that Management Banquet Night.

Bethlehem Steel had influence in the Lebanon City Council as well, at one time. They wanted to keep all the other industries out. In other words, City Council would vote against any industry which would want to come into the Lebanon area—zoning variances, things like that. One was Armstrong Cork. The council voted somewhere along the line that other industries weren't suitable for this city of Lebanon. See, we were only a third-class city.

Q: And why would they do this?

Well, Bethlehem Steel was the dominating power here in this town. In other words, they were the big employer here in town and they wanted to keep it that way. Bethlehem Steel had twenty-one hundred to twenty-five hundred people. Other industries might take Bethlehem Steel employees away, because they would give better benefits and better pay. They had the connections and the pull to go ahead and do things to any competition. For example, the Lebanon *Daily News* was right behind them to support them too. So you might as well say that they coincided with each other.

Here at Cornwall mines alone, they had a lot of jurisdiction over the borough at one time. Anything that the borough would ask, the company would provide for them such as equipment or anything like that they needed. Consequently, they did have a lot of power here as working in the borough.

Mike Stefonich

Q: How did Cornwall get to be such a big borough?

Well that's another interesting question. What happened was Rexmont was part of South Lebanon Township, one of the largest townships in the county. And the people in the area of Lebanon controlled the township and they were raising the taxes. Bethlehem decided to develop what is No. 4 mine, which was in South Lebanon Township. The Brick Row (in Rexmont) was a dividing line up there by the railroad track. So to evade that thing, Bethlehem Steel arranged to incorporate. They got enough people in Cornwall and Rexmont to sign a petition incorporating the borough. Also, many of the people in that area wanted to be part of the borough. And this happened May 26, 1925, because it was my first desire to run for council at that time. I started working for election then. And I put notices up in the mine. I was running for councilman. By golly, I got called to the General Manager's office. He told me that this thing is like a three-legged stool—government, the people and the management. He says, "Bethlehem Steel wants it this way and that's the way we're going to do it. You can run some later time, but right now we have the people we want." And they wanted to set up the borough according to Bethlehem's provisions to avoid paying taxes to South Lebanon.

And the borough benefited. For example, we have beautiful schools, we always had good schools. Later, we had a professor from Lebanon Valley College who was principal here. He had been a professor there, and he was making more money in Cornwall teaching our high school. Bethlehem Steel was the majority taxpayer. They paid ninety-five percent of the taxes in Cornwall Borough up until they closed down. In fact, I was a member of the council when the millage was two mills for the sole reason for building a nest egg after the company was gone.

71

Laying the Rexmont water main on Water Street, 1930s.

John Yocklovich

The company created many of the problems themselves, which led to the union. You got to give respect to these guys [the miners] that come from nowhere. See, we lived in the company homes; you know what a company town was at first? That was rough!

The water line was running eight feet away from my house—a great-big water line but you couldn't get no water. The real-estate man wouldn't give it to us. So what happened? I went to see Mr. Peterson. I went up there and talked to him, and his wife was in the other room. I asked him to help. I told him, "Well, Mr. Peterson, I hate to do something like this—come up here in your house and talk business like this." I said, "You're always busy when I go to the meetings about it and Mr. Hyle can't give me no satisfaction. He just puts me off and puts me off." I said, "I just decided I was going to come up to your home." He said, "There's nothing the matter with that. You can come up anytime, Boopa." "About this water. There is a big water line running eight feet in front of my house. All these people down through the towns, those poor old ladies, go out there early in the morning. The hydrants are froze and the ice is accumulated on it and you can't get no water. Some women are pregnant. If they slip and fall, what happens?" Mrs. Peterson heard

72

that and she said, "You'll get water, you'll get water!" What happened then? We got water! They put a spigot there. This happened after '36 sometime, or '38 sometime. I got the water. My neighbor said, "That will cost us a dollar more rent." I said, "Joe, what's the matter with you?" He said that will cost us a dollar more rent. I said, "Don't talk so dumb. Don't talk that stuff and get it around. Maybe they'll raise it. Don't be so foolish." But then one day they came here and they were digging down through. The people wanted water, everybody wanted water. Anyhow, Mike Stefonich come there and Joe Palmer is out there; Yaaky is out. "Well, Boopa, you got your water, that's a good thing. I'm glad to hear that. And he told Yaaky a joke. "Boop's the man that got you your water here." But we got the water!

Lester Yorty

When I first started work here on a spring day, I didn't understand many things. I was just a youngster of, say nineteen years old. The first thing I noticed was three or four of the old laborers walking down the track, going home with spade shovels on their shoulder. Oh well, spring gardening is coming up; they needed a shovel! So, many a time fellows would ask, or sometimes if they needed something for around the house, they'd take it without asking; but nothing was ever said. I know one of the railroad foremen; he said two dozen shovels he got and he went to Mr. Entrican, who was the supervisor. "Mr. Entrican, I ordered two dozen shovels and I don't have a one to show for it." Paul Entrican would say, "It's springtime so they needed shovels, so order two dozen. Maybe they will let us enough to do our work." The company took this position where they always looked down and away from fellows that took things off the job for purposes of doing things around the house. They didn't call it stealing, as long as they didn't sell it for profit. As long as they didn't do things like steal it for a profit—why it was O.K. Old Kepner, a supervisor, was quite a character. A fellow went to him one time and said, "Mr. Kepner, could I have a shovel?" He said, "How long have you been working here?" "So and so many years." "If I find out you take a shovel, you're fired. If you don't have enough sense to do like the other fellows when you need something like that, be man enough to take it and walk the hell off. Don't come to me!"

When they were tearing down the old Robesonia place, they had big half-doors for bringing things in. They had gondolas to load up for the Robesonia furnace. At that time they had an agreement with the Freemans, or whoever sold [to] Bethlehem Steel, which said Robesonia should have ore. They worked a certain portion of the open pit and should have ore as long as "green grass grows and water flows." You might've heard that saying. And of course when Robesonia did close down, Bethlehem did buy it away from them. But he went and asked a fellow that I liked, who was in charge at that time, why they were dismantling most of the things. He then asked whether he could have them doors. Kepner said, "No, I'm not going to give you permission to take those doors." It's the same thing. If he wanted them it was up to him to get them.

When they started No. 3 mine, Kepner and a lesser boss was walking around the place. They came across an electrical cord about fifty feet long or something; it was maybe a pretty good cord, a brand new one. He said to this lesser boss that I told the boy he couldn't have it. The under boss said, "Gee whiz, I could use that cable." "No, no, don't take that. We just got it. You take that, there will be trouble. We ain't done using it. Wait till we use it for a while." The next day or so they walked around, and the cable was gone. The lesser boss said, "Now, damn, why didn't I take it? I didn't take it. Somebody else got it." And Kepner looked at him and said, "I got it." He done it as a joke, but later told me, you know, "Yorty, if I would have told him and he would have got caught with it—." At that time they had security officers walking around, half paid by the government and half paid by the management. Anyhow, he said, "If he would have got caught, he wouldn't have said that he took it. He would have said so and so, the boss, said I could have them. So where does that let me?

The Second World War changed a lot of things. There were a lot of fellows from the Coal Regions who were bootlegging up there, you known, on their own development—getting coal out. And they would take powder, take fuses from here and use it up there. Of course, on account of security and things like that, the company came to us and said, "Look, where we did it in the past, it was O.K. Because of the war, a man caught taking powder and fuses—anything like that—is liable to lose his job." And we went along with it because of security and all.

Albert Perini

It didn't matter what had to be done in the borough or something like that, Bethlehem Steel done it for us. That's one thing I've got to say; Bethlehem Steel helped the borough and the people in it.

I would go to work at seven to three, and they would be concreting sometimes. We had to work overtime sometimes to six or seven o'clock at night. And some fellow would come up and say, "Hey, Albert, I'm laying a walk. I need a yard of concrete." "Are you going to be home?"

"Yes." So then when we got almost filled up, someone would call up and say, "How much you need yet?" Well, if I needed two yards, I would say, "Send four up." When we were filled up, then they would call up and say, "Albert, there is concrete left." I would say to the truck driver, "You have concrete left there. Take it to such and such a place. Take it to that house." The guy would get his concrete done for nothing. If they asked, we'd always give it to them.

We had a tool room underground there with different kind of bolts. If they were doing something at home and they needed bolts, I would say to Irving, "Give them the bolts." What the hell! They would get them anyhow. If you didn't say they could have them they would take them.

We would have a meeting about the United Fund in more recent times; they always wanted us to have a good record, you know. Then I'd tell the guys, "Well, they want ten dollars from you." Well, they bitched like hell, you know. I'd say, "O.K., just you bitch but when you want something, well." "Yeah we know, Albert." Then we hit on the idea of fixing stuff for the men. We had a mechanic on shift. The men would come out with anything from home. "I'd say, "Bring it up, even the electric bill." That's one thing they couldn't say—that we didn't do things for them. If we didn't have anything, I'd say, "Go up to the warehouse at Bethlehem Steel and get nails, bolts, anything you need." You'd ask the bosses and they would give it to you.

THE COMPANY AND THE UNION

Mrs. Warner Franklin

I used to go up and babysit for the general manager. His wife was telling me one time that she was going to take me up and register me to vote. I told her, "I'm not going to register Republican. Anybody isn't going to tell me how to register." I said, "You could take me up there and register me, but I'm going to register the way I want to." And I did. So when I used to go vote, the company people used to say, "That's funny, your husband is Republican and you're Democrat." "Not for anybody. We're different people. My husband is an individual and I'm an individual." And I registered Democratic. And one time at school, my son had on a Roosevelt pin. Some talked. I said, "Sure, he had on a Roosevelt pin." I was a Roosevelt person, that's why he wore the pin.

I remember when the union got in. The general manager of the mines at that time thought a union would never get in there. The general manager told me one day—he said, "There will never get to be a union." I laughed to myself. Even the head man at Bethlehem came down and wouldn't believe it. There was unions everywhere, and this little town wasn't going to stay out of the union. That was fun; I liked that. I like excitement.

When they organized that time in the 1930s, Pinchot was governor of Pennsylvania and his wife helped unionize United Factories in Lebanon. Mrs. Pinchot used to put on a red dess and come down and get in the picket line in Lebanon. She had the nerve to do that. It was a mess in there, because Lebanon turned factory. That was a factory place. You know some people just are in a rut; whatever is there is right and they don't want to change.

Cornwall was very hard to organize. They were about the last ones that got into the union. It was a small town, you see. One trouble with organizing was this place. You heard about laying off anyone when things were running? Well, we never did stop running. Cornwall was a good place to raise a family at that time. There was no shutdowns. Maybe things was slow—they just weren't selling ore, or something like that. But people always worked here. They didn't shut down like Steelton did. Steelton is always shutting down, always did—laying off and shutting down. But they never done that here. They have to have the ore. They didn't have to use it here; they used it in Sparrows Point, Maryland. They used it wherever Bethlehem Steel had plants, you see. There was too much money in that place to shut down.

The other problem was that Bethlehem Steel owned everything around here at that time. They didn't sell or nothing. We had better schools here; we didn't have as much taxes. And they were running everything; they was paying for everything.

The Depression

Bethlehem Steel enhanced its stature in Cornwall during the Depression by aiding its employees in a number of ways. Primarily, the company "carried" people rent free in its houses. Mike Stefonich and Lester Yorty recall the tremendous relief of people in the borough that they were allowed to remain in their houses. For others, the company used its influence to secure federal jobs. Most grateful were Mike Stefonich and Albert Perini, who secured jobs, respectively, with the PWA and the State Emergency Relief Board. When the Depression was over, Bethlehem Steel willingly took all former employees back on its payroll, in part to help them pay back rent.

Mere residence in Cornwall often was enough to get families through the Depression. Besides the rent-free homes, local merchants—especially the Freemans—often distributed free food and carried most on credit until after the Depression. Large gardens, willing neighbors and other community resources helped.

But the depth of suffering and humiliation occasioned by the Depression can best be measured by the fact that many now refuse to talk about it at all. Many people were hurt, physically and psychologically, by its humiliations. The very conservative culture of Lebanon County was especially damaging, since the people in relief agencies in the county tried to pin the blame on the victims of unemployment. Russell "Red" McDaniels' interview is a moving, evocative document of the toll the Depression and the acceptance of relief took on his family. Confirmation of the humiliations and privations "Red" McDaniels' family suffered is offered in Albert Perini's interview. Especially illuminating is the role of the lady in the relief office, who personified shame and defeat. Who, in Lebanon County in the Depression, could forget the picture of her looking at license plates to determine who deserved relief and who were "free-loaders"?

Russell "Red" McDaniels

We were poor. I would say that because when you walked in the bread lines during the Depression days, you knew you didn't have something to do. My dad put me in front of him many a time to go to welfare—what you call the welfare. But in them days it was public assistance. Then you would wait in line for your rations—bread and sugar and butter and stuff like that. I did that many a time with my dad.

My dad was laid off from Kaplan Brothers in Lebanon, where he was a crane operator, around 1932, '33. That's when us boys went out and took the load off. From then on my dad didn't work hardly at all. My two older brothers and myself helped out. Where Cleaver Brooks is today used to be a big scrap yard there, where they made a lot of shells for World War I. We used to go out there and dig this up; it used to be a scrap yard years ago and then they tore it down. That was all a vacant lot there where the Cleaver Brooks is today. And we would go out there with our wheelbarrow by day and dig this scrap with a pick and shovel, fill it up, and take it to the scrap yard. And that's the way we earned our money.

Though my dad didn't work again normally, he did get a position after a time with the WPA during the Roosevelt administration. Mostly he did a lot of work at Coleman's Park, which is a memorial park today. That's where they had the guys out there fixing the roads up and fixing the buildings and stuff like that. That was one of the last jobs my dad had—WPA. I'd say this was about '36.

The WPA worked this way: they said they were going to take you off the welfare so that you would have to go out to work. In other words, you weren't on welfare anymore; you weren't on public assistance. If you had a WPA check coming in, you couldn't get public assistance then. In other words, you worked your public assistance off. And they got you on WPA.

Mrs. Weber was head of the welfare—public assistance. I was young at the time, but she was kind of a go-get woman. I mean she was a very bossy-type woman; people that worked for her didn't care too much for her and she seemed to be really an authority all the time. I don't know how long she lasted there, but I know there was some criticism against her—Mrs. Weber. I remember that good. She could put a knife in you and have no compassion whatsoever. She was a tough old woman.

Well, then in 1936 the funds ran out for a while. Then they got it back in but they called it another system. They didn't call it WPA anymore. It was Public Works program or something like that.

But Dad quit before I graduated—1938, 1939. He hurt his back and he never went back to work after that. Now he hurt his back to the extent where he wouldn't even go to the doctor. He was one of those bullheads of a father. You know how they are; and that's the way it was. And he didn't go to the doctor's, and five years later he died. He had what you called peritonitis. I guess today it's the same thing as cancer just about. But then I don't think from around '38 on till '45 did he work.

Q: How did your family put food on the table after he was off the PWA?

In 1936 both of my brothers started working at the concentrator. They got me through school and fed me till I got out of school and then we put my other brother and my sister through school by all going to work.

Peter Rossini, Jr.

My dad got a little relief but not a lot. And I'll tell you it was tough sledding. Some storekeeper was kind enough to keep you on a ticket, you know. But now I'll tell you who was good—it was the Freemans. That was a dairy there in Cornwall. We used to go every morning and we would get a gallon of skimmed milk for nothing. It was warm and they would skim the cream off, and they'd give you the skimmed milk. In the summertime they had peaches at their farms; they'd let you pick peaches off the ground. They helped the people along, regardless if they had posted the land against hunting or anything. They were good I think. Well, from North Cornwall and Burd-Coleman we all went over there for milk; probably Quentin went too.

Hopkins, the butcher, carried us on credit. They would give the people credit. When you would settle up on payday, that's when you got a couple of candy bars. Candy was scarce, too, you know. A nickel was a big item. We ate groundhogs or anything during the Depression. Many people ate groundhog. If you haven't lived through a depression, you don't know what it is.

I graduated in '33 and I couldn't get no job here. But my uncle was working. He was a manager at a cheese factory in Wisconsin. So he had a job for me. So when I graduated I went up there to Wisconsin. I was up there for two years or so working at a cheese factory for $45 a month and board. And that wasn't your clothes. That was just sleep and eat. But I tell you, I worked every day. You had a half a day off every two weeks. And you didn't know how long you was going to work, especially in the wintertime. The snows would get deep and the milk trucks wouldn't come in on time. When they did come in then you had to work up the milk. So I put in hard work up in the cheese factory. Then I came home. My brother was in the CCC Camp. We thought we could find work here.

That was in '35. The mine wasn't starting up yet. So we went back to Wisconsin again to the same cheese company, up here near Minnesota. We were there about six months and then we got tired, and we come down.

My brother got a job at No. 4 mine right away in '36. And it was November before I got a job. I didn't want to go underground. I wanted to go to the open pit. I saw this Entrican, the boss, every day. I was there every day looking for a job. Finally, in November I got the job. I worked about a month and a half tamping ties and putting in ties on the pit railroad till they started the shovel up.

Matt Karinch

You couldn't get a job then anywhere; you just couldn't get a job. So I fell in for this one—indexing the books on one of the government project jobs in '34. I was on that till they were finished. I was one of the last to get off of that job. That was when Roosevelt, I believe, got in. It was a white-collar job. This was the CWA (Civil Works Administration). It was one of those jobs and I had a tough time getting it, too. I went into Lebanon and applied and I didn't hear anything. I saw that a lot of people were applying for that job. Some of them had fur coats, and at that particular time they were applying for that job. I knew some of the people that were going there, and their families had what I considered a lot more than me. I went over and I didn't hear anything so I went back to where they were hiring and I said, "I didn't hear anything." I went in and I sort of told them. I said, "I'm qualified to do this work. If I don't get a job, I'm going to find out why. I'll write to Washington." I believe Mr. Hopkins was in charge of that at one time. And I said, "I'll write to him and tell him I was turned down." The fellow was from Schaefferstown who was in charge of the Lebanon Branch. He was hiring them. Then they called me and I got in there. I was one of the last to get off. At that time they were getting somewhere around a dollar an hour or something like that; that was a good job. We only worked like five hours a day. They had two shifts—either twenty-five or thirty dollars a week. That was good money at that time. Then in '35 I took over the hotel.

Mike Stefonich

I worked for the State Emergency Relief Board in Harrisburg. They only had 150 people working on that board when I started in 1934. They had over fifteen hundred when I left. You had local offices and you had Harrisburg. They grew like mushrooms. These people on government projects had to get paid.

80

We audited the doctor bills. For example, when they delivered a woman for $50, there had to be ten visits; and the sixth one was with the birth. There were five prenatal visits, the delivery, and four after that. These would make up $50. We audited. We made sure the doctor followed the procedure. If he didn't have four visits down before the delivery, he didn't get paid for those. He got paid for the delivery, which was probably $10, and then the postnatal cases. You had those ten visits to get $50. There were contact people in smaller towns which handled the cases and sent them to Harrisburg. But the invoices went directly up to Harrisburg. All the bills to be paid were paid out of Harrisburg. I don't believe the local offices paid their salary. I was up there on the payroll department at first. Then later on, after that got straightened out, I got into auditing these cases—bills, doctor bills and so forth.

See there was so much work at SERB because everybody was out of work. Lebanon was a steel town, as it is today. Bethlehem Steel was the biggest employer; and then we have the two foundries and a boiler works and stuff like that. Everything was shut down in Lebanon. They had food distribution centers set up in the county. We had one in Cornwall. Mr. Peterson was manager at Cornwall and he suggested to me that I go up to one. I said, "No, we're going to try and make it without it." I didn't want any help from anybody. I'll pay for what I get and I don't want it for nothing. Well, they gave them each a bag of flour, you know; we didn't even get a bag of flour. They were handing it out to you and said the government was paying for it.

If I hadn't gotten the SERB job I'd probably, for a financial reason, have gotten a job at $5 a day. I was sitting here at first not doing anything. I have a family to support, indirectly; it wasn't my family, but my mother and my sisters and brothers. I had a nephew living here. And we weren't on welfare. I wanted and insisted that I get something, to Mr. Peterson. So he said, "I have a job open in Harrisburg for you. We don't have anything here." I didn't want a road job because I never could work on the road. I said, "No, I never did road work and I'm not going to deprive some fellow that could use that job. Why should I take a job in a field I'm not experienced and capable of doing?" There was a job in Lebanon County Courthouse getting $5 a day. It wasn't much of a job though. This other thing in Harrisburg was much better because it opened up a new field for me.

When I come back later in the thirties as Rent Man for Bethlehem Steel, I found that the company had been carrying a lot of people. There were a few who couldn't pay cash for rent during this period. What happened when the mine started up was they all had bank accounts and we had an agreement with them that they would pay so much on their back-

Miner's Village, late 1930s; company store on left.

log. We would give them periodic statements and tell them just what their balance was, and they had an idea when they were paid up. It was set up like with my father going to the grocery store and buying on the book. In fact, they still do that up in Miner's Village at the store. The man has a book and the people buy something and mark it down. He marks it in the book and then they pay him periodically. Some will and some won't. But most did for the company. But to me the Depression was May 1, 1932, when I lost my job, till when I get that job in Harrisburg—maybe until 1934.

Lester Yorty

The Depression hit us pretty hard and we ran up a bill around two hundred and some dollars back rent for Bethlehem Steel's home we lived in, and we couldn't see to get clean. We were working maybe two days a week when we moved here. Then it got progressively worse until we got laid off; I would say, around the end of '32 it was shut down, finally. The Depression was the only time I couldn't get work.

Then I got work at the Lebanon Steel Foundry. I worked there for six months. Then Mr. Entrican, the boss, came around and he told my wife that I could have my job back. They would call the maintenance men back to work first so they could get the plant things ready. Then they would call back the other people as they needed them, like laborers, brakemen, firemen or whatever you had shoveling. So he came around one afternoon and told my wife my job was open. He knew I was working at the steel foundry; and if I didn't come back they would give you so much time, then they would terminate you.

I liked it at the steel foundry. I liked the working fellows. But like I told you, they had periods of shutdowns there too, according to how orders were. Fortunately, I was working the graveyard shift, from twelve to seven, or something like that. Nobody else wanted it; the seniority guys didn't want it, you know. We were working in there and some of them were being laid off. I went to my foreman and I said, "How does it look for a fellow to keep a half-decent, steady job?" He said, "Yorty, I can't answer that. You know how things are. Right now you're working because nobody wants the late shift. I don't know how long." I knew this myself; I shouldn't have asked the question, so I figured I might as well go back to Cornwall, where I more or less had steady work until the Depression.

Albert Perini

During the Depression on government projects, sometimes we only worked three hours in a day. If the concrete-mixer broke down they wouldn't pay you. Some nights I would come home at ten o'clock. I had five hours work from the morning.

Q: Who paid your wages?

During the Depression they called it the welfare. It was through the welfare department in Lebanon, but this contractor from Williamsport had charge of it. The lady from welfare was the head of it locally. You went over to Lebanon and they told you where to go. These two friends of mine from Cornwall got a job over there. The one guy was a serviceman; that's how he got it right away. The servicemen were first. And then I seen Donner (a friend of mine who was a serviceman) out here and I said, "Hey, Sam, get my name in." He told the welfare lady and the welfare people said, "Bring him along." Then I started over there on PWA on different projects.

If you had help from your parents or you owned your own home, you would have trouble. I want to tell you something. We'd go to town once a month. So one Saturday morning in 1934 we went to town—Hilda and the kids and my mother-in-law—we parked the car in front of Pomeroy's Department Store in town; the welfare lady came down the street and looked at the license number, checking to see if it was my car. That's how they did it in those days. She checked it out because we would have been getting charity. And they figured if we had a car, we had enough money. She wanted to know if the car was in my name.

The funny thing was that favoritism had been going on all the time. There were many cases! One of the fellows went out to welfare and got any damn thing he wanted. He got so much stuff that the kids used to throw it away. And another fellow would go in there and hardly get anything. Right after the Depression began, I had a friend of mine in town who worked there in town giving stuff out. He said to me, "Albert, how are you doing?" I said, "Nuts, we don't get nothing out here!" "Don't you, Albert?" I said, "No." "You come into me next week," he said. "You write down what the hell you want. I'll fix you up." And I got called back to work then.

Work, Safety and the Union

The work in the mines was demanding and dangerous. What made the job bearable was the comradery which developed in work gangs. The men kept up their morale by playing practical jokes and by giving each other nicknames. Some foremen were very popular and were well known for their pranks and their sense of fair play. One of the best and most popular foremen was Albert Perini, whose rise from the ranks also epitomized the second generation ethnic American's move into a position of importance between labor and management. His interview only hints at how difficult his job was in the mines—a consoler of the men, a confidant of labor, and a man ultimately responsible for production.

But no matter how good the foremen were, tales of disaster and death were at the back of all the underground men's consciousness. Part of the problem was the process of underground mining—boring under the ore and blasting shafts up to the body. In these interviews the problems of this kind of mining surfaced only when John Yocklovich and Albert Perini discussed the methods and terminology of mining—what a "raise" is, how shafts are sunk and the ore body "undermined," and how a miner "scales" a roof. Complementing the discussion of the dangers involved were astute observations on the absence of even rudimentary safety equipment in the 1920s, 1930s and even 1940s. There were no steel-tipped shoes, no "hard-boiled" hats, no safety glasses, no respirators, and no real first aid. Though safety equipment was not introduced into many industries until the 1940s, this did not mollify the Cornwall laborers.

Another problem which contributed to accidents was the sheer exhaustion of the men. Men in this kind of work just wore out in their fifties, but could not retire. As Albert Perini relates, "pensions" were inadequate and insurance amounted to little more than a couple hundred dollars. Consequently, there was no financial security and the only recourse was to continue working.

In the face of such problems, the natural response was collective action. Lester Yorty's experience, revealed in an important interview, is representative of many actions taken in the open pits before serious attempts were made to unionize the Cornwall mines. Work stoppages could occur over any number of important issues: unfair wage scales, grievances over firing, safety problems, or even the payment of back rent for company housing. There was little fear, in reality, of resisting perceived injustices before the 1930s.

The company union and Bethlehem Steel's paternal concern proved incapable of dealing with the tremendous dissatisfaction and insecurity stemming from the Depression. The issues in Cornwall were primarily safety, hours of work and, almost incidentally, wages. The disgruntled workers of Cornwall found ready allies in the Steel Workers Organizing Committee's (SWOC) representatives—the Garby brothers—and in the miners working in the pits who had come from the Hard Coal Regions. These hard-coal men had had years of experience with the United Mine Workers, and realized the value of a powerful national lobby.

Even with deep-seated grievances and willing allies, the "union" men's first attempt at organization in 1937 ended in failure. The major problem was Bethlehem Steel's agreement with SWOC; the SWOC organizers in Lebanon County were restrained from using all their resources to organize Bethlehem Steel. Other difficulties presented nearly insurmountable odds against organization: the competition of the teamsters for union membership; violence toward "union men" because of ignorance (many in the county believed the union men were involved in a conspiracy to undermine public order); threats of the loss of jobs; and, especially, the inherent conservatism of nearly all the native-born workers. It wasn't until 1943-44 that serious work stoppages and the pressure of the federal government made it necessary for Bethlehem Steel to recognize the union.

THE WORK: UNDERGROUND MINES

Albert Perini

Q: Can you remember that the men held you in esteem? That they treated you differently in the sense that you would deserve their respect? Did they tip their hats to you?

[Laughs for a while.] They never tipped a hat to me. But they were all good to me. I was good to them and they were good to me. Once in a while you would have a run-in. But if you had a run-in with the guys, you would forget it then—forget the damn thing and be done with it.

I had one man up here that worked for me. He was a hell of a good worker; but he did too much as a miner! He would work like hell. But he was sort of like this steam kettle here; he wouldn't say much and he couldn't think too much. But he always got his work done. And then when we would go down in the morning, there was one guy on my shift that never liked to work with him. And then I used to call this guy [the hard worker] over and say, "Hey, when I ask you who you want for a helper this morning, you tell him you want Engels." Bugs Engels they called him. "Hey, Willie." "Hi, Albert!" "Who do you want this morning?" "Give me Bugs!" I said, "O.K., here's Bugs." And everybody would laugh, you know. They would laugh and this guy [Engels] would get mad. He didn't want to work with this head miner because he didn't talk too much or anything. He just kept working.

See, the problem was quotas. When I first started working as a fore-

Shift foremen at No. 4 mine, Cornwall, 1940.

man in a production outfit in the thirties, they would look for at least fourteen hundred tons an eight-hour shift. Well, there was a little bit more to the quota then because we weren't down in the mines so far. See, the further down we went, the longer it took the skip to come out. See, when we first started, hell, you could just cream it off the top. Later on it took longer. We had delays, too. The skips would jump off the track and would knock a hell of a lot of steel sets down, you know. Then they would take sometimes a whole shift or two shifts to get it repaired. But if they got fourteen hundred tons, they were always satisfied. This one guy didn't get fourteen hundred and maybe the next shift got sixteen hundred.

Q: Did you have times when you weren't making your tonnage?

Oh yes. We had trouble. If we would run into trouble, I had to report it. If the hoist wouldn't be running, I would check for time and how much. Then I had to write down, "Thirty minutes: hoist delay." Sometimes on Saturday nights and Sunday nights we would be short of manpower. Some guys would stay home. Well, that didn't hurt us too much. There wasn't that many off at one time—maybe one or two guys. We always had extra men, and then we used them up for what they were needed for. Sometimes, however, there was just me and who else on the whole line, two guys for the whole mine.

Q: What part of your work force was foreign-born?

I think at first we had more foreign-born than Dutch. Towards the last there was more of the American-born of foreign-born parents. Well, you take years ago [1920s]; in that open pit it was as foreign-born as hell because the Spaniards [Mexicans] and all were here. Then they sort of left somehow. See, they shipped them in. A lot of them died off and went home.

We didn't have too many colored. We had our hometown colored. These colored guys that we had around here were nice. They were brought up with us and we played with them. Goosetown had the Franklins. Then Butch Hays. And Bunch Burrs. That's the only colored families in Goosetown. Brick Row had none. Miner's Village had a couple of them. Burd-Coleman never had too many; there were more foreign people there. North Cornwall had a couple and that's all. Then we had some from the South—Dewey Murphy and them. Mrs. Franklin must be eighty or more and they also came out of the South.

I was one of the foreign-born. They called me "The Big WOP." I said, "Just don't call me a Honky. I resent that." Whenever the telephone would ring I would say, "Hi." They'd say, "Is the Wop there?"

Underground miners, early 1960s, Earl Kohr in center.

"You're talking to him. What do you want?" The men would call up on the phone sometimes. The older men didn't like to be called names. I never called them guys Honkies. But in place of that they all had a nickname. One guy was called "Teeth," and one guy was "Lemons." His name was Leaman, but we called him Lemons. One guy was "Tomatoes," because he raised tomatoes. They all had nicknames. Why you wouldn't up and call someone a "Honky."

And the foremen! There was more foreign-born foremen than the Dutch. Then there were the superintendents: Mel Lipensky, Paul Entrican, Arthur Peterson, Nathan Brown, Joe Barnhart, Mr. Shale, Mr. Olson, Kepner and Bingham. They weren't foreign-born.

When I worked over at the No. 3 mine, we were always after each other. Years ago they had this baseball ticket out; you know, they used to count the runs. If Chicago had four, and if you had a four number ticket—if that matched up—you hit the 500. They used to sell them that time for fare. This was years ago. So I always had to go out and get the baseball scores at seven o'clock. Then I would come down and these guys would look at their tickets. One time I saw this guy's number ticket; so I come down the next night and I said, "We'll fool him tonight." I come down and read the things off. "I got it, Albert." I said, "Do you? Let's see." We checked and I said, "Dang if you didn't hit the $500." "Call up my wife, call up the Rexmont Hotel, and tell them to send two cases of beer down to my house. We're going to stop and drink it after work.'' Well me and these three other guys stopped there; we drank his beer. The next morning he got up and went over to see the main guy that was selling these tickets. ''Hey,'' he said, ''I got the number last night.'' ''Did you? Let's see.'' ''Yeah.'' The ticket seller looked then and said, ''Hell, you don't even have the number.''

Q: Then what happened to the guy?

All of us guys laughed.

John Yocklovich

Q: What is a raise?

I'd say it was a four-by-four board. You drill and blast up through rock, straight up. You make a shaft. I went up to 185 feet, straight up. Then I could put my machine and stuff in there to drill. You would go straight up in the air; you would make your own shaft, straight up in the air. You blast four foot of rock down at a time. You put a stage in with the oak poles. A stage is two poles across—and then you put plank on. Then you stand on this again and drill with a machine that weighs about 175 pounds. As you put raises up, the shaft went down one hundred, one-fifty, two hundred, two-fifty feet. That's how they kept going down until

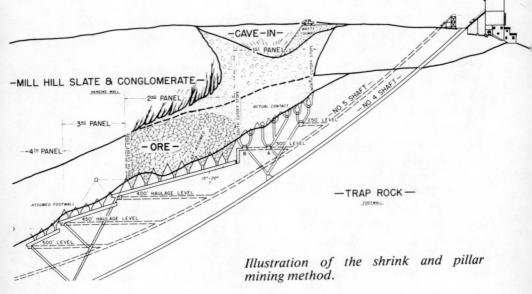

Illustration of the shrink and pillar mining method.

Underground miners drill in No. 3 mine, Cornwall, 1936.

they went down twelve hundred feet. You thought it was only fifty feet from one-fifty to two hundred; but it was more than that. It was a big body of ore. Twelve hundred feet is straight down a shaft. They put a shaft that deep, twelve hundred feet straight down, but it was at a 29/31-degree angle at the first couple hundreds of feet. Then they would drop a little bit and they would go down to about a twenty-two-degree slope. It sort of flattened out down there at the bottom. You drilled a shaft up maybe twenty-five or thirty feet because there is rock before you hit the ore.

You will be sitting down there someday and one of them will be running good for you and the other side won't be falling there yet. Pretty soon you hear it good—"bloop": chunks are falling down. You can hear them fall—"bloop." That's falling down all night and all day long. It has to. If that wouldn't fall down there it wouldn't be safe in that mine. In other words, if you have a big area like that—say you take a half a level and you have a big area—then when that would fall down, it would kill every man in that mine. There'd be a concussion; it would blow you up. It would take all the oxygen away from you. But that was cheap mining. They took these shafts clean up to the rock. If it was two hundred feet they took it clean up into the rock. But that was too high to go up. Bob Weaner had to come out. From then on they watched it; they

91

didn't go up like that no more. Everybody chewed the fat about that; I know I did myself, as far as that goes. But them long holes were great-big. On my God, that was a good method. We didn't get the ore like we should've but I thought it was great for the working man.

WORK AND SAFETY

Albert Perini

In the 1930s they had a lot of trouble in safety. Well, for one thing we didn't have our hard-boiled hats. It was way after the thirties, you might say, that they came in. You didn't have the hard-boiled hats, and you didn't have your hard-boiled shoes. You know, with the tips? They didn't furnish you with gloves and eyeglasses—safety glasses—years ago. And then when this come in, if you got caught without your safety glasses on, you'd lose your job. The reason for it was the company was getting a lot of these accidents. Then they finally did something. At first, in the forties, we used to have a safety meeting every month. You had to have a safety meeting every month. Then we would get to talking about different things and finally they appointed a safety engineer. He worked in the main office. Then he started getting all these things here; we had to get safety glasses, etc.

In my experience, the men were a bit careless in the early days. The guys didn't seem to think like they do today. They didn't give a damn about nothing. After we got stricter we had safety meetings with the men and all. Then we got to explaining and then they watched more. You know, they watched like hell what they were doing.

When the union came in in the 1940s they wanted safety. They wanted to get these goggles and everything like that for the men, and safety shoes. Before, I had my old canvas cap. If you got hit on the head it would go right through. Now these hard-boiled hats, they save your life you know. One time I got called in the mine—it wasn't my gang since I was over at No. 3 underground at that time. I was just working at that time and a guy came around and said, "Don't you blast!" "What's the matter?" "Some men are covered up, up here." "Aw, go on!" "Yeah." "Where at?" Some of us guys went up and you couldn't see them. A big, big lump of ore just pushed them straight down into the ground. Then we had to get jacks. There was four men working together there and these lumps fell down and it just ripped the other two men on the shoulder. These two men who survived were wild to see that their two buddies were under there; they were killed right out. That was about one of the worst accidents.

92

In 1929, that's when the mine blew up—when the shots went off up here at No. 4 mine one time. That was right after we got married. We just began living out there in Rexmont. There was a thunderstorm around six o'clock. Now Boopa, my brother-in-law, was working that night. He related this story: One of the guys heard the shot go off in the mine. Then the one guy said to the other guy, "Gee, they're blasting early tonight!" Well, they didn't think anything of it. The guys were eating dinner. The men wondered where the men setting off the shot were. They didn't know. Then Boopa and those guys walked up and they said, "I smell clothes burning; rags are burning." And the smoke. They could hardly get back to the place in the mine. The two men's heads were off; there was nothing but a little bit of their bodies laying there. They were loading a shot. Now, they don't know if the lightning from this damn thunderstorm could have gone down through along the rails. I think that in loading the shot the cap must've been sticking out of the hole a little bit, and they hit it too hard with hammers and it blowed them to pieces.

Handling powder is dangerous! Don't let anybody tell you it isn't! Any kind of a bump with them caps and—. That's what I said before; they would send powder down and the guy would just grab the bag and throw it. They didn't give a damn in hell if powder like that goes off. But them caps are the main things; when you stick that cap in that powder you better be sure that you have it in the center. If it sticks out a little bit and you put it in that hole—. You always got to tamp them so they stay in solid, you know. If it isn't solid then the shot doesn't break. But if you tamp it like, and that damn thing sticks out and it hits that rock—a little bit of a spark—that damn thing will go off.

Q: Now, what happened to the people who had somebody die in their family? Did the company give them a pension or did they have compensation?

You were covered with insurance. Now this is in 1963. Back in the thirties you only got a couple hundred dollars when you died. Mostly like a burial! There wasn't much the widow and children could do. Florence Carpenter went to work. She also was on that charity business in town. If you got killed in the mine, though, they go so much for the kids and all. It wouldn't be a whole lot but it would be something.

People worked long because pension back in the old days paid so little. Look at the old guys that worked in the mines, who walked to work and worked ten hours, and would walk home again. When they retired, if they got $30 a month, they were rich. Thirty dollars a month! I know that's true. I used to deliver the orders for the storeman. He would give me the checks and put out the money—$28 and some cents most got a month in pension. And we couldn't understand why they didn't keep their houses! My God!! They would've been eligible for social security but there was nothing like it.

John Yocklovich

I'll bet I learned fifty guys how to mine. But first all the miners learned underground mining off of Rossini and the other guy, Louie Colon. See, Colon was the other boss. He went to the coal mines, too. They were all rough guys. Don't forget it! All they believed in was drinking. When they started drinking they'd drink for a whole week.

Q: Weren't they afraid of accidents?

No, they didn't think of it. There was no safety gear then. When this mine first started we didn't have no safety engineer. No goggles, no hats, no nothing. Carbide lights. They're dangerous but we used them; nobody ever got hurt with them. And afterwards [1940s] they got a safety engineer and then you got your hard-boiled hats. And then you had to wear safety goggles. Then the company went for it because if they had an accident it was against the company.

At first the only thing they learned you to do was to scale your roof and how to salvage.

Q: What's scaling your roof?

It was the first thing you did. You trim the loose stuff. You sound your roof with a pick. If it sounded hollow you knew there was a crack someplace, and if it sounded solid you knew it was good. If it's hollow, get it down, it's loose; put timber up there. There weren't too many accidents for the mining method at that time. But the worst accidents happened in the thirties when they got too close to the rock. See, when they got close to the rock they should've left that go so many feet from the rock. That will give every time. That will peel off; ore will peel off of rock. You know that it don't take much for that ore to fall, that was as heavy as hell. You had a lot of men that wouldn't work underground.

Lester Yorty

Q: What kind of a safety program did you have?

When a man would get hurt at the mines, we were trying to get an office or dispensary out here where you could get more help. I mean they had some things—like cotton, tape, bandaids, iodine, some grease and things you could slap on yourself. Or they had a guy who was supposed to be maybe a Red Cross guy and had some experience; but they never had no nurse or anything like that. We were at least shooting for a nurse. And the final judgment on that was, "Look—when we have a serious accident—until we bring that man out from underground, and we know that he possibly will require a nurse, doctor, we'll call the ambulance and get the ambulance out at the same time they have him out of the ground. We can load him up and take him into town." That's the way they answered that. We wanted to have more localized dispensary to take care of fellows that got hurt on the job. We had quite a few accidents.

John Yocklovich and Albert Perini

John Yocklovich: We didn't know any better about working so hard. We were taught young. You know how we were taught? By our parents! And we gave our money home—my God! That was nothing else. I was twenty-one years and I gave my money up still.

Albert Perini: I wasn't quite eighteen yet, and then they sank the shaft at Robesonia to put a pump in for an open pit. Son-of-a-bitch, but didn't this Paul Entrican, the boss, put me on with these old miners from the No. 3 mine. They were older than I was and I was a young kid. We would go down and they would blast; one guy would do the drilling this way. You helped him to get started. Then the other two men over here would join in. I had to muck out [clean up]. But they blasted the whole shift. We used to get sixteen or eighteen mucker cars a day, shoveled by hand. Everything was pick and shovel at that time! No machine! Nothing but shovels in my day.

John Yocklovich: That shaft that we sent down for No. 3 was something down there. By God, when you come down there, it was only twenty-two feet by eight feet. The minute light was shut out there, you saw that pile of ore. My God! They had those little, short shovels; you would stand on your head, on a twenty-nine to thirty-one-degree incline, and you shoveled. Our feet were on the wall. You were on a degree and you had to shovel it and you had to throw it up in the car. You got organized; you done it. The boss was sitting on the step looking at you. If you rolled a cigarette too long or something, look out! He'd say, "Hey, what's the matter?" We used sixteen to eighteen cars on a shift. We were taught to work. You had to work to earn money; that's what we were taught and that's what we do to this day yet.

95

Peter Rossini, Jr.

So I was on the shovel working in the pit, carrying the timber up, and jackhammering. That's one problem with the hearing. When you're jackhammering rock, you didn't have no ear muffs or anything. I'd put cotton in sometimes. But when you're drilling rock, you get more of a pinging noise and your ears would ring a couple of hours after that. Ore didn't ping as much as rock did, you know. The only thing with ore, you had to pull your drill up and down, otherwise the ore would cake up. When you drilled at night you had to have a couple of spotlights on the shovel. But then at night you don't know what's coming down over the bank when it's dark.

I never wanted to go underground. Now my brother was afraid of height actually. But when you put up a raise [a platform in one of the shafts], he wasn't afraid then because he couldn't see the bottom a hundred feet down. Then it was dark.

I didn't mind heights. A lot of guys wouldn't even go up on Shovel #9 in the open pit. When I first went up they had the ladder on one side and the other side didn't have no ladder. Some guys got dizzy; they went so far and they were afraid. But one of the bosses showed me. We used to have to repair that shovel then, like put wire plates in. You had to crawl over to the other side where there wasn't any ladder. Then you had them little pockets, and you had to crawl from one pocket to the other to put your bolts in and hold the wire plates in. I could crawl anyplace on that shovel there. The boom was ninety foot long, pretty high there. I wasn't afraid as long as I had some place to hang on. I wasn't afraid of height.

You heard about accidents all the time, underground. One fellow's dad was killed over here at No. 3 mine. Down where the old shaft was there was a bridge frame on top. On this bridge they used to have sand bags or stone bags piled there that they used for concrete, or something like that. And he was coming up on the skip. Usually when they're hauling men, they have like a stud thing that they slide into the slip to sit on like a ladder. When they put this ladder on when you're coming up, you hang on the top of it instead of sliding down to the bottom. So he was sitting on the bail and one of these bags had dropped off the bridge down on the track. When the front wheels of the skip hit it, it worked like a dump truck. The bail lifted up and pulled the back end of the skip down. Well, it throwed him off and I guess he broke his neck.

Russell McDaniels

Q: What was it like when you were going down in No. 4 the first day?

Underground in No. 4 mine, Cornwall, 1950s.

Well, first of all, I got off at 500 level and a guy says, "You go with this man here." His name was Jim Smith and he was a head miner. I said, "O.K." He said to me, "Come on, son. Come on, I'll take care of you." He was an old-timer in there and he took me back. It was all dark back in there. Now he said, "You watch yourself. You fall down one of these holes or something and I won't be able to find you." And he tutored me just like a father would and that's the way I did till I got hurt. I was working up for him in '57 till I got hurt. And then I went on my own in '57, '58, '59. I was on my own then and he still was working there yet. Like I say, he tutored me good and took good care of me.

The first week that we got there, they asked for miner helpers. Frank Mahalic wanted me to get on the timber gang with him. But no, Ross [the boss] put me with Jim Smith. So that made me a miner helper. That's better than being a timberman. So many of them got injured by lifting heavy stuff down there—lifting timber; if you didn't watch yourself you'd get hurt. Timbering was really dangerous, and you had to go in the dangerous areas to repair it. The miners didn't go in there because they had to go in after it was repaired. But the timberman had to go in first. So, like I said, he sent me with Jim Smith and he had us together, I don't know how many years. Then they put me on my own until I got hurt. Then I had a helper for all them years. When I got hurt, I came outside and I couldn't go back down any more.

97

Where we worked—even if we knew the area was bad—we knew we had to go in there and do it. Lots of times we didn't have the right equipment to go in and clean this area up good before we could start timbering all over or start drilling and blasting all over again. By the right equipment I mean the right protection mostly. One time—I think when we started here—I don't even know if we had respirators. In other words, you eat all that dust while you're drilling. Later you had water machines which took away that dust, and then you wore a rainsuit. And then, still later on—in years to come—they gave you safety glasses. Lots of guys got pieces of something in their eyes. We got better stuff in the fifties. A lot of new safety protection came into the mines only then; we did have hard hats.

THE UNION

Lester Yorty

What I wanted to say is how easily you could get marked in those days. You know I told you that I had come from Philadelphia? Well, these fellow workers around here thought that by being from Philadelphia gave me ins. You got more pull, something. So they used to say, "Hey, we're going up to see management." At that time it was old man Sowers. That would have been in the 1930s, before I was in the company union, before we even thought of having the union.

Anyhow, we wanted to go for more money. Like with the railroad—the difference was only seven cents between the workers. See, that's the way you graduated up to becoming an engineer, a brakeman; then you fired, then you became an engineer. So they tried to approach Sowers a few times and they always lost their nerve at the last minute. One would start out, and two would drop back, and after a while you've lost everyone. [Laughs.] Nothing happened.

Anyhow, I was putting water in the tank one day. "Hey, Yorty, we're going up." So I said, "As soon as I get the tank filled, I'll be up." Like I said, I was young. I could get around like a whippersnapper, if I have to say so myself. So before Sowers came down—when he seen the group coming up from the railroad track—I was up there. Frank Whitman was up there. So, all the shovel men and other guys seen us. From the pit down below you could see the men watching, and they wanted to see how we made out. After they seen we weren't getting fired or getting whipped or something, they would come up and join us. They were down there. So poor Mr. Sowers came down. He was down there across the street; he was at the gate. They had called the main office at the time, and he said,

"What's going on? What do you want?" And words to that effect. Like I said, I was the last one up, and I only knew in general what they wanted. I was no more of an agitator than—. I wouldn't want to name who started the thing. I wouldn't have known. But, when they asked questions I felt so sorry for him and regretted the inability of them answering him in kind. So I told him, of course. When I spoke up Frank Whitman came and helped me out. From that time on I was an instigator. If it hadn't been for my wife's father being a foreman—we were living with him at the time—maybe I would have had some different experiences. I don't know. But you have to stand up and have the courage to say what you want. We got a little pork barrel.

My being from Philadelphia did help a bit with Sowers. It made me see more of a democratic way of doing things, a human way of doing things. I won't say I thought this way at the time. But looking back I can say it helped me. You know you're worth your salt. If you don't know what you're worth, you won't get it.

Around the time of the Depression we had the company union. You had to go to the main office and talk to Mr. Peterson, who was the general manager at that time. Anything you wanted, like flour, shoes—you put in a request. If they had it, I guess you got it. They'd get supplies, allocations from Lebanon or something like that. So a lot of these foreign fellows started to ask Mr. Peterson when he made these visits, "How about the rent?" See, no one was working; no one was paying on the rent. And no one got throwed out. Peterson would say not to worry about that, they'll take care of it. So when we went back to work the company went around—they knew how much each one owed. Some would owe a thousand dollars or more. But to everyone they asked—they didn't say how much you had to pay, they said, "How much do you want to pay? How much can you afford to pay that back rent off?" I know some paid as little as fifty cents a pay. At that time we got paid the first and fifteenth of the month. It was not exactly every two weeks. So, when we had the company union, the question came up of why we have to pay this [rent] back that Mr. Peterson said the company would take care of. We had a fellow in labor-management and he finally wrote a letter to Bethlehem. The fellow that was with me and myself representing the workers said, "We'd like a better explanation to what Mr. Peterson said and why we have to pay it." So he wrote a letter and he left us read the letter. The letter said, "Mr. Peterson maybe said he would take care of this. This is the way *we're* taking care of it. The use of words, the interpretation of words is misleading as you ought to know. You can say things, and maybe you say things knowingly and want them to think that. But in your heart you mean something else." So, that's what happened there.

99

Mike Stefonich

The Bethlehem Steel strike started, according to my records, on March 4, 1937. I felt sympathetic toward it because it "will reflect an improvement locally." Now as you probably remember, I told you that President Roosevelt had indicated that people should be paid $5 a day. Now this is what they wanted, and I showed you on my paycheck what I was getting at the time. And that was the reason for the strike. Now my part was rather insignificant in it in that I was part of the management. Later on I had to work. I recall distinctly after the strike got going that Cornwall men were induced to strike. They already had the union in Lebanon and they were organizing the union in Cornwall. Remember, John L. Lewis was the high muckety-muck and he was organizing the union. He was President Roosevelt's right-hand man, you might say, as far as labor cases were concerned.

There was a CIO, in those days the Committee for Industrial Organization. They came out and Mr. Peterson was, as I told you before, flustered because he didn't know how to handle labor. He was a mining engineer. But rather than fight them, he shut the mine down. So as far as the operation was concerned, other than the caretakers, nobody worked. The office force, including myself, worked all through the strike. It lasted maybe two weeks. It isn't like today—everybody had a different way of going in when you picket in front of the gate. In those days it wasn't enclosed with a fence or anything. And people from Burd-Coleman would cut across the hill over there. People from Miner's Village would come their way, the people from this area (Cornwall Center) would drive to the parking lots or walk as they got there. But you all got to your job in the pit. In other words, it wasn't difficult to get in.

Well, anyway, a day or two later after shutdown things were getting rough, and then I had to learn how to operate the switchboard. I was single at the time and the other two people were married; I had to work one night from eleven to seven, so that we would have somebody on guard. We had police officers who patrolled the mines to make sure that everything was O.K. When someone called for help I would contact the proper people. But that only lasted one day, and then they got over that scare. I don't recall what happened after that, but the union came to Cornwall. Mr. Hyle became the management representative and I was his clerk.

And we had terrible times. The union, as you probably are well aware, had demands which were outrageous and, of course, the company wouldn't agree to them and we finally compromised things. They wanted the privilege of buying gasoline at the storehouse like the office employees and the salaried employees could do. And, of course, this would have entailed quite a lot of bookkeeping process. As it was there was only about a dozen or a dozen and a half people who had these privileges. They wanted to buy safety shoes and equipment and they didn't want to buy it at stores. They wanted us to sell them to them—the safety equipment to them. The company had to have a storehouse. I don't know how they settled up, now. But those were the types of demands they wanted. And, of course, they had complaints against certain supervisory people who did things that were obnoxious to them. So these were the type of complaints they had. The basic wage was set at a higher level. U.S. Steel had an established level [which established the pattern for the industry]. But it was never on a high rate of pay. I don't think I ever got much. My highest wage which I got was $61.41 for two weeks. We never got the wages that we deserved. That was ten days of work. They eliminated the Saturday to work so you worked five days a week. It became a custom to work eight hours and to provide more work for the people—to share it around. And it was an established policy. Up until that time Cornwall operated on the basis like it always had prior to that. You worked ten days, ten hours a day. We, in the office, only worked five and a half days a week. See, as an office employee, I got off at Saturday noon.

After the strike, we got the five days a week and the men got the five days a week. Bethlehem Steel, prior to this time, had a bonus plan. If we produced over a hundred thousand tons of ore a month, we would get a bonus. And sometimes that bonus amounted to $12 to $15. But you had to work in the period in which the bonus was created. It was a tricky plan.

Later in the forties, they got the people to join the union. Now, they had one fellow in here for the union. But he was as radical as all get out! He made people nervous. My boss, Mr. Hyle, by that time had become a cigarette smoker, and he smoked one cigarette after another at meetings. These Kool cigarettes that kept you cool. And the room was filled with smoke. He got sick later and then this fellow Kepner took over for him. And I got out of it then. I didn't have to sit on these employee-management things, which was good. And later on, of course, Hyle got out of it, and Charlie Neil, who's now the company's representative, came in. He's one of the later breeds. He was trained to look out after his company problems, locally now.

Russell "Red" McDaniels

In '37 I recall that my two brothers were working at the concy in Lebanon and the State Police were riding horses up and down the concentra-

101

Union hall, Lebanon, after fire, 1950s; Irwin Carpenter and "Red" McDaniels, left to right.

tor path waiting for the picket lines, waiting to bust up the picket lines. The State Police were going down through with horses and busting up the picket lines as they tried to form. Some non-picketers were trying to get in the gate and work. I recall that.

I remember later on when the first union really came into existence with Mr. Phil Murray. They got the charter in '39-'40. That consisted of Bethlehem Steel and the concentrator and the mines at that time. The steel foundry didn't come under that charter. This was called the United Steelworkers of America and Bethlehem Steel was part of that. All its subsidiaries were part of that—the concentrator, the mines and the big plant in town.

Q: Do you remember how that was organized or put into effect?

Well, yeah. You had to sign a card whether you wanted the union in or not. You signed your cards at the plant.

Q: Was there a Steel Workers Organizing Committee, a SWOC here in Lebanon County?

Oh yes, they had one at 134 Cumberland Street, a place they called the

Union Hall. And that's where the members would meet, and they would put a yes or no on whether to go out on strike or put money into the union and keep the union people going so they wouldn't have to go on welfare or anything like that. In other words, they had a fund set aside.

Q: Just like a strike fund you mean?

That's right.

Q: And what year about was that hall opened?

The picture in the hall down there with Philip Murray is 1939, but the full force of the United Steelworkers, which is one and a half million people, went into force in 1940. That was the real pack of 'em.

Q: Did this committee have a hard time beginning in '37 in trying to organize?

Yes it did.

Q: Why?

Well, there were too many wishing to organize. There were other people that wanted to organize the steelworkers too. One was the teamsters. They wanted to get their foot in the steelworkers' contract and some of the unions fought against other unions at that time. Our scuffle was with the teamsters. The United Steelworkers belonged to the CIO so that gave them a boost in power.

Before this they did have what you called a company union, but you couldn't say anything yes or no on their plans. But the company union would set the plans out, so you would know whether you worked Good Friday or you wouldn't get paid for Good Friday, or the holidays or Christmas. You didn't get paid for it; that was their plan.

But when the union came in they revised all that stuff. There were two organizers, the Garby brothers, who came from Virginia and organized the concy and the mines up here. It had to be outsiders though. Later on, after the mines were organized, they went back to Virginia. But the two Garby brothers helped to organize this Lebanon area for the Steelworkers. They set up a committee right here in Lebanon in 1937-38. Eventually, we had different locals. Our local was #2657 at the mines, and their local at the concy was #1231.

Q: Was it a real struggle to get the union established here at the Cornwall mines?

Well, I didn't work here before the union got in. But some of the stories I heard are something; they throwed paint all over your cars and smashed your windows and it was real rowdy at some times, I understand. Those who did it were most of the people who didn't sign the union cards and wanted to work.

Q: What did they have against the union?

Let's put it this way: I would say maybe they didn't understand the union at that time and I think maybe the company had them brainwashed at the time. They didn't like what the union was doing, maybe. I'll tell you why. If a man went home from his job in the early thirties, he went home from his job and he was told by the foremen, most likely, that if you go union, don't come out to work no more. You're done here. Well a guy couldn't afford to lose his job. So the company threatened them many times by saying it would fire the men if they went union.

So, in order to go union they formed a union committee and a grievance committee, and different kinds of officers made themself staff and everything else. They would set up the program for the people. The orders came from Pittsburgh. They would set up the program and they would send down here what to be done and what not to be done. They would pass this card out to you. Then they would say, "Here, you know your wages are lower than so and so wages and your fringe benefits are way below anything else. Your vacation, you don't get half of what some of the other plants do." They would write this stuff down that you don't get things, and here's where the union would help: "You go union and I'll help you get them." The committee would endorse it. You can't fire none of the men who work here. There was some threats, but not to the extent where you had to have any kind of protection. You know what I mean? But many non-union people felt we were a conspiracy.

These people wouldn't ever sway to the union. So when they got the union in here—the first contract you got—you didn't have to belong to the union if you didn't want to. But you had no rights to some of the overtime or holidays, or whatever. You didn't have no rights. The union people were the first to get that. I would say at that time, before I started here, lots of them didn't want to join the union.

Q: What were the issues that were important?

Well, first of all at that time there was just one week vacation out of a year. There was no such thing as sick leave when we started—I mean paid sick-leave benefits. There was a variety of benefits they were never getting. One of them was higher wages. They were getting $1.78 an hour or something like that.

There were other, not so immediate, benefits. Take some of your widows today—they benefited through their husbands being in the union

104

that got good insurance coverage when they passed away. Also they got compensation when they got hurt. Three-fourths of that check, just about, was coming in every week while you were laid up on crutches or whatever. That's where the family benefited from it and not just the individual that worked there. The family, his children and the wife also got help.

And the union helped lower-level company people too! Don't forget it! Every time the union would get a new contract—a wage increase and more benefits—the salaried people got the same; they all got the same. So they didn't lose nothing out by the union. I heard it said that foremen didn't get the full benefits of management but they benefited more from the union. That's true because they said the working man was getting more holidays than the foremen were getting. So the management gave the foremen more holidays.

Another thing that happened was better safety. That was the first thing and we began to have classes on safety. They gave us two hours off to maybe go outside and have a class in the shower houses before we ever would go down underground. They would talk about safety and they had safety engineers. As soon as something came up you would report that to the safety engineer. He in turn would send out the electrician who is responsible to fix it, and things were kept in good shape by doing that. It made foremen's jobs easier.

You must realize that we generally liked foremen, but some of the workers didn't. The main reason for hostility was that some of the fellows felt there was favoritism. Some of these fellows that came in from the farms browned up foremen. Not some of the local ones; it was some of the farmers. They did come in and give chickens and potatoes and a lot of groceries that they had growed on their farm to the foremen. The foremen would make their jobs easier, whatever their classification. If they were timbermen, they had to timber. That didn't make it much easier, but he could put him in an area where it was less dangerous. If he didn't like me he could put me over in that other area and do the work over there where it was more dangerous. But some of them did show favoritism in the mines, yes they did. The union didn't get involved in that point of view or the controversy. When it comes to that, that was between the foremen and their help. The bosses' protégés were mostly the Dutch people down around the Schaefferstown area and Prescott area. There was a lot of people who kept their farms going while they worked here. In other words, they asked to work night shifts—all night turn, eleven to seven—so they could work their farm during the day.

The last union picnic we had was in 1970-71.

As I said, some of my buddies on the floor didn't like some foremen.

They got up on the floor and said that no foreman's invited this year, and that hurt a lot of people. I liked foremen and they liked to come out there. Albert Perini was one of them. He loved to be with the gang and sit down with the men and talk.

Earl Kohr

The union men from Lebanon wanted to get as many men signed up in 1942 before they had an election; they had to see if the union was represented. And they would come out during the week and talk to the men over loudspeakers. Then they would sign them up and you paid a dollar a month. They were from the steelworkers union in Lebanon. And they would have a staff man there. A lot of them guys from the Coal Region that come down here, I guess, were the first ones to sign up. They were John Rubright, Russ Rubright, Ollie Miller, Joe Garvin, Ralph Light. They came from Tamaqua and I guess up around Minersville. They came down here for jobs. I guess it was around '37 when the mines really started up again after the Depression—in '37 and '38.

I remember the one time when they had a strike in 1937. They had a picket line and the one guy tried to come through. They got a little rough there; they threw paint on his car and everything else.

Seniority became an important issue; it wasn't that way right in the beginning. When the mines first started up, there really wasn't that much of a chance of being laid off because things were going good at that time. Then during the war and everything else, they really had good going.

In them early years they mostly wanted you underground. They didn't want you outside. They wanted you to go underground right away. Very few people got a job and stayed outside. They wanted you to go underground. I guess they figured that they could get anybody to work outside. But many didn't want to go underground. They had special people that stayed outside and they couldn't go underground. Maybe they had something wrong and they let them out in the open.

The union was concerned about accidents. The mines are high risk. Some people were killed and others were hurt. I believe a lot of this happened before I went to the service in '42, soon after I started working in the hauling strip. See, at that time we had like ten by ten timbers setting up maybe every five or six foot apart. And then here is like a space where you could get in between. When the train came by, the train caught my bib overalls and drug me in around the train and the timber—that ten by ten timber—and then I was in the hospital for a little while. So I got alright then. But they were pretty good on safety after the union came in. They had a safety director and everything.

The End

While the company has done a good deal for the villages, a few miners point out the very real problems left by Bethlehem Steel which the borough to this very day has not yet solved. On the positive side, Bethlehem Steel remodeled the company houses it owned and sold them at a reasonable price to the occupants, established a water authority and brought water to the villages, donated buildings and land to the borough and religious groups, and left surplus funds in the borough treasury.

There are two basic problems: an inadequate sewage system and an inadequate tax base to support needed improvements. In other words, the problems remain, primarily, because of the void created by Bethlehem Steel's departure. There was simply not enough money from real-estate taxation to support needed municipal improvements after the company pulled out.

Charles Neil's interviews should be read very carefully. His remarks are very important since what he is talking about—imported ore replacing Cornwall ore, the mobility of capital, and the high costs of domestic labor—forms the substance of the national debate on deindustrialization, the dismantling of our basic industries in the United States.*

Locally, the most obvious effect of the shutdown was the immediate loss of five hundred jobs. But there were other problems over the long run which no one had anticipated: the inability of many miners to secure and hold new jobs; the difficulty of attracting enough industry to replace Bethlehem Steel; the departure of sons and grandsons from the area; and, in general, the end of a whole way of life.

*For background, the interested reader will want to read Barry Bluestone and Bennett Harrison, *The Deindustrialization of America: Plant Closings, Community Abandonment, and the Dismantling of Basic Industry* (New York: Basic Books, Inc., 1982).

Russell "Red" McDaniels

The '72 Hurricane Agnes finished us. And they went to push the auxiliary pump on at the 820-foot level to help the 1,225-foot pump room because it wasn't taking the water out fast enough. It was raining in too fast in Hurricane Agnes and going down the shaft. The pumps went off at 820. See, they were already grounded before they pushed the button for that and the water kept coming up. Till about five o'clock that evening everybody was out of the mines. I was on night shift that week, but the day turn at five o'clock had everybody out.

Q: Did you have a feeling then that things may not get back to the way they were? Did you have a feeling that they would close down?

Oh, yeah.

Q: Was there a rumor going on for a long time or not?

Well, actually, the mines were going to shut down in 1980. There was notices and rumors to that fact in 1968 already—that the mines were going to shut down in 1980. They were depleted. They said the iron ore is there yet, but it's costing more to get to mine.

Retirement party for John Yocklovich, seated center, 1968. Brother-in-law Albert Perini stands to his right.

Q: You mean it's down deeper?

Not only that, you have to go through more rock to get it. So, in other words, it took maybe two more weeks of working to get to that ore. It is good and rich once you get it, but it is costing more as they go deeper and deeper.

To find out what you have you have to drill maybe three hundred feet before they took any ore out. It was a diamond drill, which is one of these—that's what you call coring. Now that's rock there. When that came out on a diamond drill set and it came out with ore in it, then your engineers would see how much ore lays behind that three hundred foot of rock. Then the miners, after the diamond drillers would get these, would get the coring out. These big, long boxes would have the cores. They would find out where this streak of ore is at. Then the miners would go in and dig this out. They would go in and drill and blast.

It was one of the engineers who was pessimistic. I think his name was Leet. He was saying at one time that the ore was rougher to get out. It's getting harder and harder to mine everything. He didn't say that we were going to shut down, but then the rumors did fly right from the top office that the mine was going to be shut down in 1980.

Q: And this began in 1968?

Yeah, about '68 or '66 already with notices about the mine shutting down.

After the pumps went and the mine flooded, it just knocked eight years off their prediction, because they had to shut down in '72. So, in other words, the Hurricane Agnes just shortened the mines by eight years by flooding it out.

Q: But yet Bethlehem Steel still has mineral rights around here?

Oh, definitely. They own all the mineral rights here. They sold every piece of land here there is and they gave Cornwall Borough acres and acres of lands for recreation. They sold the open pit to the Sheraton Slag Company for a dollar. These buildings over here all belong to the church home across the street. The concentrator now is getting tore down section by section. [The last of the concentrator was removed in early November, 1983.] The homes in Miner's Village are all owned by the people who live in them. But three foot under their cellar the stuff belongs to Bethlehem Steel—all mineral rights.

Q: Why's that?

Because they want mineral rights in case they ever have to come back there again to get it. They would have to tear your home down, but they would have to give you the value of your home. They could tear your home down and dig under your cellar because they know there is ore under there. Some of these old-timers around here say there is an abundance of ore here. But, like I say, it is so hard to mine. It's so costly to mine to get to the ore before you're making any money.

Q: So the price of ore would have to go way up?

I would say.

By the way this all had a lot to do with the union. In the late sixties, that's when they wanted to change seniority for the power of layoff. That's because the mines were getting down to the point where they weren't going to be any more. They were always talking that they were going to run out of ore and that they were down as far as they could go. Then all the miners were changed to belong in one unit. It must've been around the fifties that they sank the No. 4 shaft down deeper. And then in later years they weren't going down any further. They were running out of it then; that's as far as they were going to go. That's the late sixties. That's when we made up our mind to get straight seniority. So the company really wanted to have the separation between the outside and the underground.

THE COMPANY

Charles Neil

Q: How did you insure continuous production?

Well, the object was to get as much as you could. When I was supervisor in the underground mine in the early 1940s, the attitude, of course, was a little different than it is today. Lack of productivity is what is ruining the United States completely. It appears that the more money people receive for their labor, the less they produce. In those days the production people would use a piece of chalk. For every trainload they took out and dumped at the pocket, they'd make a checkmark on the locomotive and try to outdo the ones before them; they had a rivalry going. Well, they can't do that now. Then, if they got out thirty railroad cars of seventy tons a car, well we're going to get out thirty-five! The fellows worked; they really worked and they weren't getting much of a bonus. The attitude changed as the years went by.

Q: You didn't even have a bonus system?

No, we never did.

111

Q: Never?

Never. And there weren't any quotas set. You got as much done as you could. Actually, the situation was such that nobody pushed and tried to make them get another load out. And there could've been a lot more production than what there was; but that was the way of life.

Q: O.K., you indicated that there was a change in philosophy. It would seem to me that what you're saying is that a person would actually work less to earn more in recent times. Did you notice a change of philosophy at a certain point as far as labor relations, the work of supervisory people, in safety, and so on?

You could see it. There wasn't anything you could put your finger on except that you knew the results weren't there. And, I told you we closed down the Grace mines and we closed the mine in Canada, although there wasn't any lack of ore at the Grace and Canadian mine. I explained it to the union that we were finding that we could import ore from Venezuela, Sweden or Liberia cheaper. They would rail it from wherever they were mining to the seaport on ore carriers, ship it to Philadelphia, load it into railroad cars, and take it to the Grace mines or take it to Cornwall and make pellets out of it at the same cost as mining it at the site. This is what we were faced with at the end.

In the early forties, between '41 to '45 when I was in supervision, our employees were producing an average of eleven tons of iron ore per manshift worked. Now that's for everybody in the mine, not just those that were in production but the development people as well. At the Grace mines we went from the same mining methods we had here to a mechanized method of mining. I think a couple of times they produced seven thousand tons at the most in a ten thousand-ton-per-day-capacity mine and plant. When they closed down the Grace mine thirty-some years later, they were producing 10.6 tons per day per man. We were producing manually eleven tons per manshift per day thirty years earlier. You can't survive like that.

We said to the union we can't afford it. See, we were tied in with the steel-plant labor unions. Typical was the last negotiations. I heard them say, "Well, the company that can't afford to do this, pay the price, or to do that should go out of business." We did! And thousands of people lost their jobs because of this. There was no real remorse. Now they have a clause in the agreement as of last summer that you have to give them a ninety-day notice of your intent to close an operation so they can argue with you to try and stay open. After we were closing here in 1973, the union came here and said, maybe we ought to talk. I said, "About what?" "Well, perhaps we could operate the plant and get a different wage structure."

112

The problem was always productivity. At a major contract signing several years ago, I. W. Abel, the Steelworkers president, said to his men, "You're going to have to produce more to pay for the concessions that we got—the increases in wages and all the other things and the pensions. We persuaded them to give us these benefits, so now you're going to have to work for it. Productivity is going to have to increase." It was his brain child, his idea, that labor-management productivity committees be established at each operation.

Q: Did it actually increase productivity?

No.

LEGACIES

Earl Kohr

After shutdown some went to Steelton, some went down to Morgantown, some went into Lebanon, and then whoever could take pension, took pension. They were taken care of because that was in the contract. If there were any openings, they had to offer you a job with a certain amount of pay if the other place closed down.

The concentrator reopened in 1974 because there was a demand for the pellets. In fact, I could've come back after I was on pension. They called me back but then I had a job down here with P.R.L. Industries; that's where the machine shop was. The Brenner Machine Company was in the storehouse for the mines. And just the other week I was laid off down here. They cut down to one shift of welders. See, we did a lot of nuclear work down there. Since Three Mile Island it really went down. It's picking up again, so I probably will be going back to work.

Q: At the end when the mines were closed, was there very much hardship for the borough itself and all the different villages?

I guess the taxes went up. See, when the mines were going they had to pay a percentage of taxes and stuff. Why, I guess they paid on whatever they got out.

I guess some people had it a little rough, too. When I retired then I didn't do nothing for two years. And then later on after that I went back to the textile. I went back to where I worked as a kid, at the new place— Jimmy Hansford's. It might've been a year or so I worked and then the slack season came in there. Then I was laid off in there and then I got a job out here. A little while later they called me to come back in the mines and that's when the concy was starting again. I had three places to go to work and so I stayed down here. Now, I'm laid off down here.

113

Q: How did the borough or Bethlehem Steel get the new industries in here?

Through the Redevelopment Authority too. We got a pretty big loan from them.

Q: Are there any problems you know that might remain from the old days?

Oh yeah, they have a sewage problem here. In fact, they are talking about getting a sewage plant in. They have this land thing down here now, right down here near the ballpark, right around the curve. They are working on it all the time. You can smell it. There are backups down in Goosetown. They're still talking about putting the sewers in like every-place else, a plant. It will cost because they're scattered out in different villages too much around here. Did you see how it's filling up the pit there? The mine pumps aren't keeping the water down. The new sewage system will cost. In time to come the state will require it.

These problems will not be our problems. Years ago everybody knew everybody in their little town here. Right now the older people are selling their homes off and new people are moving in. Some people live here who I don't know what their names are.

Charles Neil

Between 1941 and '43 the company spent several million dollars on the 219 homes that the company owned in the Cornwall Borough of eight communities. They put in baths and they put in central heat, and fixed up the homes. When I took over in '54—the real-estate responsibili-ties—the company was trimming the hedges and collecting the garbage twice a week, without extra cost to the tenants. They were painting and papering and repairing the furnaces or doing anything that had to be re-paired. And when we began to sell the houses in 1957 the average rent was $21 a month. And then we decided to sell the homes to the tenants, whether they were employees or not. They began the program in 1957. I sold the rest of them about six years ago. But the homes in Toytown went for an average of seven thousand dollars or seventy-five hundred dollars. And the ones in the villages went for $4,100 a side for those beautiful one-hundred-year-old stone homes. Before they did that they replaced the water tanks with a steel water tank addition, placed water meters in all the homes, and built a new reservoir. The old one only held seven hundred thousand gallons of water, at the lower end of Miner's Village. Then a water authority was formed and they turned, I think, the whole three or four hundred thousand dollars over to the borough. But it was in the '41 to '43 when they changed these homes that the people stopped their gardening. Maybe it was the improvements, a new generation, etc.

Cornwall is still very pleasant to look at. It's not a crowded place to be in because of the company and there is a lot of history here. The people are generally friendly and yet it is one of the biggest boroughs in the country—it's about six and a half miles in diameter. More recently we have these new housing developments—Springhill Acres and Ironmaster Acres—on land which Bethlehem sold to the developers. I don't know what the population is now, but it must be twenty-seven hundred or something like that. It used to be twelve or thirteen hundred.

There are other legacies, of course. Of course, I'm prejudiced because I've worked here for forty-four years and know some of the things that the company did for the borough. Some of the little things turn out to be big things to certain people. For instance, the black community, which is located in each of the villages except for Cornwall Center, was given the old grade school at Burd-Coleman. The company had given them half of that and they used that early on as a church. That's the Baptist faith. We had a very good relationship with them and we let them do what they wanted to do with it. We helped them fix it up. When the time came, we gave them the entire building for the traditional dollar. The Mennonites were up in Miner's Village in what had been an old boarding home. That's the big framed building on the right as you go up to Miner's Village. They were willing to buy that. I persuaded the company that we should give it to them, too. So we gave them that building for their traditional dollar. The state got the charcoal furnace from Mrs. Buckingham. We repaired a lot of things in there without charge.

More recently, just before I retired, we gave the borough all the recreational lands—all the land up here across from my home in Anthracite and up in Miner's Village. That's twenty or twenty-five acres of land for recreation. The things that we did with the water system, the improvements of the homes, the low rentals, and again the low sales prices for the homes so they could own them. You would think that there would be a situation in which the company would be held in high regard and so forth.

There are a few people who get up in the public meetings and condemn Bethlehem. We're supposedly responsible for all the evils of the town and all the problems that were created for them. And in the minds of a great deal of people here they have some very hard feelings toward the company. It's almost a case of what have you done for me lately? But there are a lot of other people that have moved into the community who never knew Bethlehem who also criticize the company. I suppose there are more of them than there are the old-timers. But I can't understand some of the old-timers' attitudes. Some of them admitted that when they had a job with Bethlehem and made good money with Bethlehem they didn't really appreciate it. They would crawl back on their hands and knees now to have a job here again if they could. It's a little too late for that.

But Bethlehem Steel was a government itself; it's encompassed so many parts of the people's lives, such as housing and employment, recreation, town government. It does seem to resemble the federal government. People here expected it to go on forever, and they felt betrayed when it didn't. Well, you see it was natural for that to happen. But some of the newcomers tick me off. Because of their education and so forth, they got on the borough council, got on the school board, and maybe swayed a lot of the decisions. These people never knew us. You don't even know who they are; there are strangers on the borough council. They get up and publicly condemn the company.

Q: These people from the outside?

Yes, and of course the young people.

And then the flood came along in June of 1972 and destroyed the power and the mine flooded again [it had flooded in 1936]. And the water came up within a hundred feet of the surface of the shaft, and it resumed its normal water-table level. Springs were flowing again, the ball field got sloppy and muddy and the septic tile field started floating a little bit here and there. They claimed that was all Bethlehem's fault, of course. They had a state geologist, and they hired a consulting firm to come down and examine the whole thing. The fellow [the geologist] got up in public and told them this wasn't Bethlehem's fault; this was just nature restoring itself to the normal water level. And, oh, they just ripped Bethlehem apart.

Bethlehem did so much. Why it was traditional in Cornwall to get company equipment. In the summer they got pointed shovels to spade their garden and in the winter they got the flat ones to shovel the snow. Within reason the company did do a lot of those things. If a fellow needed some boards for something, he got them. We had a carpenter named Jim Alwein who charged a fictional account for materials and supplies. He had a charge account, a number that he made up. When somebody got a piece of lumber or something for nothing and they'd say, "Jimmy, what's the charge?" And he'd say the usual, "Account #B-one-eleven-nothing-nine-C."

You've got to remember supervision's changed. When I first went to work the superintendent was a man named Howard Kepner. He was the bull of the woods. He would come swinging his arms and be livid with

116

rage. He would start chewing somebody out in a hurry. But when the times were slow he took the workers and went over to the Boy Scout camp and planted hundreds and hundreds of trees up there in the mountains. We planted pine trees; we kept them busy at the company's expense.

They did a lot of things, but some of the stuff comes back to haunt you. They say that Kepner told a fellow who wanted to borrow a ten-inch wrench, "Don't tell me you don't have one of those yet!" So there was a reputation, probably deserved, that the company was lax.

* * *

The property tax structure of the county was geared to the fact that you had certain buildings and equipment and things like that that depreciated; you could see these things on the surface. But Bethlehem Steel also had an iron-ore body under the surface which added to the value of the property. As you produced the iron ore and got rid of it, then of course your value lessened. Prior, I think, to 1954 the tax people of our county and the company people got together and set up a schedule to accommodate those decreases in allowances. I believe it was in the neighborhood of a half a million dollars a year that they reduced the assessed valuation for Cornwall Borough as a depletion allowance. And as a result of that they had a schedule which was geared to the production, the normal production. It was projected that when the iron ore was all depleted, the tax structure of what was left would be at its right level and it was. That was done so it wouldn't have any sudden impact, any jolt to the local assessed valuation of the community. And it was well done and well planned. When the mine closed there wasn't anybody that felt any real severe increase in taxation as a result of a loss of that extra income.

When it ended we had left in the No. 4 mine, as I recall it, about one more year's production; that's about all. It was just about depleted, and had there not been a flood we would've closed in 1973 anyhow for no other reason except for lack of iron ore.

Q: How were the decisions made in 1972 about getting one more year of production out of Cornwall and then shutting down?

Well, the economic situation throughout the whole country changed before we shut down in 1972. The demand for pellets diminished completely. We were working about forty percent capacity before 1972. All the stockpiles at the oreyard and steel plants were filled to capacity and there wouldn't have been any place to put any more, except on the ground here. So, they decided that the cost had gotten to the point where they couldn't produce anymore. There wasn't any reason to operate. They

117

said it would be a waste to operate. Those decisions are made at the corporate level, not only by the mining department but by the overall board. Earlier the same board had closed down shipping. Bethlehem used to be the largest shipbuilding and ship-repair outfit in the country. Now they're down to two repair yards, or something like that. They have the whole picture, you see. They closed up the mines in Canada, too, because they didn't need the product.

After we closed up, would you believe that the production of pellets dried up everywhere and we couldn't get pellets anyplace? So after we had cannibalized this plant, took all the mills and everything out, we had to look around the whole world for replacement equipment. We had to go into production again making pellets. We built the concentrator up again and then went into production for three years and then closed down completely. So it's the ups and downs of the market! In other words, it turned out we closed down when we should've stayed open.

I had a hard time getting people to staff it again after we had been closed down. I had to get 125 people back. I started calling people back in August of '74. See, we closed down on July 5 of '73, never to open again. *Never, never* to open again! So we tore the place apart and shipped this here and there and sold stuff. And suddenly we had to open it up again. Most of the former workers were working at other plants, like the Lebanon steel plant, the Steelton plant. I had to get them back. I even asked the people who were on pension to come back. I made an agreement with the union that we would treat those pensioners just as laid-off people and keep them on the seniority roster, and call them back as if they had been laid off and see if they wanted to come back. These people were secure by then in other jobs. The pensioners were working for school districts or other places as maintenance people and what have you. And I'd say, "Well we need you!" See, they were subject to recall for up to five years, that is if we treated them as if they were laid-off employees. And when I called them they had to make a choice to come back or not. If they didn't come back I had to write them off and let them stay where they were no matter what. Many were new employees at the Lebanon plant or the Steelton plant. The first thing you know they'd ask, "How long are you going to operate?" I said, "A minimum of three years." "Well in three years we will have to go through all of this again. I'm not coming back." We had about 153 such employees say no. I'm looking and I'm trying to get people to come back, experienced people to staff the concentrator and produce pellets for three years.

Q: And did you produce pellets?

Yes, '75, '76, and '77.

Q: Right here?

Yes.

Q: I never heard of that before. How many people did you hire?

120 to 125.

Q: What did you operate?

Just the concentrator, now.

Q: Just the concentrator from here. And where did the material, the ore, come from?

From Venezuela and Liberia principally. They bought it where they could buy fine ore, you know. It didn't have to be crushed. We didn't have any crushing plant then. We rebuilt the concentrator beginning in August of '74. We got into production, I think it was the end of March or the beginning of April of '75. And then in '77 the whole market collapsed again. That's when we closed the Cornwall mines in July and the Grace mines in September.

Matt Karinch

The educational program [at Cornwall] was losing a lot of money on the Bethlehem Steel assessment. There were rumors that they were making a lot on gold and silver which was being mined in the borough. They didn't pay their portion of taxes for years. Some of their properties never were assessed anywhere near what they should have been. And I told them years ago when I was on council, "Someday, they're going to move out of here and leave you without anything." I fought for new trucks when I was on council. I was on for over twenty years.

When I first took over the Blue Bird Inn, we were paying about $44 a year. Now, it's about one thousand dollars. See, we were going to have a problem as Bethlehem Steel pulled out, and our taxes would really increase. I fought them when they wanted to take a bond on the school. I was just eighteen or nineteen, but I was at Lebanon Valley, and I was familiar with the way taxes worked and why they were taking a bond issue. I felt we shouldn't have a twenty-five-year bond issue. I think we ought to pay it off in a few years. "Pay it off right away while the company is paying the big taxes. They're paying ninety percent. They'll pay it off. Do it now!" Then the Borough Council took a twenty-five-year bond; they were losing half a million dollars a year by taking the bond issue. "Why spread it out when this is going way down? The individual taxpayer is going to get hit harder and harder. Let the guy with the money pay

119

for it now. Then we'll be relieved.'' The company wouldn't hold still for it at that time. At that time I didn't have the hotel. I just knew what was going to happen in the future. The problem is the depreciation of Bethlehem's property by half a million dollars a year.

Mike Stefonich

Q: Could you see that they might close down the mines?

Well, yes, in a sense you could. I was in Borough Council up until then. And one of the councilmen mentioned the tax rate was seven mills. One of the councilmen said, "This mine is going to be closed within the next few years. Why don't we raise the millage up two mills? That way we'll build a tight nest egg for after the company leaves." So, even though most of the councilmen were the company employees, they agreed to that. And the tax rate has been nine mills ever since. But the strange thing about it is, that after Bethlehem Steel left, the council passed this one percent tax, the wage tax; with it the school board gets half and the municipality gets half. Right now our tax receipts from that one-half of one percent tax is greater than what our real-estate taxes from the company would give.

Then the flood came along and, of course, you couldn't come down into the pit. The company would have to make a decision whether they would reopen it, taking into consideration from their estimates how much ore was there. It wouldn't be profitable to reopen it. They would have to recondition all the electric motors and stuff because they had all fallen under water and everything was done by electricity. For example, they had tramp cars run by electricity down there in the ore operation. They had scrapers in there that were up to the shop. They would sort of peg it into the face wall, and they would have a machine that would pull it back and forth, and they would scrape the ore to a pocket and the pocket would fall down to a hopper into the cars. It was mostly mechanical work, other than operating and running the drills, and blasting underground. There wasn't much variety to it.

I would say everything stopped in '72. It got to the point where Bethlehem Steel not only stopped here but they sold their other ore properties recently. Now the borough of Cornwall owns from the bin here, at the last house, over to where the borough garage is. That was donated to the borough.

Now, a fellow out here bought a small section over there, on Willow Road over to where the railroad still goes up to No. 4 shaft. Until they dismantle all that equipment, that railroad will go there. But I think in the process the concentrator is just about ready to be dismantled, unless some other industry moves in there. A man by the name of McMagnus bought it, and this fellow Pinchot up here is acting as an advisor in selling off the various pieces of equipment. But that still hasn't been decided. Now there's no railroad tracks to the open pit any more. Some environmental group bought the right of way in Lebanon County. They wanted to make a bicycle path. I think what they should have done is bought it and made a public road out of it.

Bethlehem stopped hiring people to Cornwall some ten to fifteen years before they shut down. If you wanted a job at Bethlehem you went to Morgantown. They have a mine down there similar to Cornwall's. My son was one of the few people they hired. Then Morgantown closed. Now these other fellows in Cornwall who lost their job in Morgantown got jobs in Steelton or Annville. Bethlehem had branches there. But it makes a long ride. Now those who were anywhere near the retirement age, they gave them the type of pay that if they stay on till sixty-five and they don't go on Social Security, they got enough to survive. Then the company will put them on a pension, at a lower rate than the present pension. Morgantown will reopen someday. There's a large body of ore over there.

There are problems caused by the absence of a good sewage system we should have put in. We made adjustments. Here, the only thing that goes into my septic tank are the two commodes—the one upstairs and the one downstairs—and our bathroom. For the rest of it, we have a separate tile field that our laundry water and the kitchen sink and the basin downstairs goes into. We just don't overload our septic tank. And I'm just a little concerned that we ought to clean it again. But there is only the two of us now. At one time there was six of us.

The company did a lot of good, though. For housing I remember when the company owned Burd-Coleman; that looked like a mess. It's beautiful now. They cleaned it up. Miner's Village is beautiful. The homes the people [have] they own themselves. They have improved them; some of them put driveways in alongside their yard because there wasn't enough room to park cars on the streets. Sometimes some of the families have two and three cars. Sons and daughters have cars. So compared to when Bethlehem Steel had it, the homes are real nice. The company sold them because the tenants were forever bitching about getting their houses fixed. Many no longer worked for the company; they bought the houses for $3,600 in 1957, '58, '59.

They were generous when they sold them. Bethlehem Steel gave them all first opportunity and most everybody bought them who lived in them. And today they're selling for thirty thousand dollars, ten times what they bought them for. But you must remember these people themselves improved them. In addition to that, the next generation is the ones that are fixing it up, not the generation that worked for the company.

The push behind selling the houses was the knowledge that they were going to get out of Cornwall. They knew just like the oil companies know how much oil is in the ground pretty well. They anticipated and Bethlehem knew how much ore was there. And any money they lost in those houses they just wrote off on their income tax. They didn't lose anything.

Closing the mine behind the last truck, June 30, 1973. Left to right are Superintendents Elso Rossini and Mel Lipensky.

Conclusion

The transition from life supported entirely by Bethlehem Steel to one in which the company is no longer present has had a tremendous economic and psychological impact in the borough. Beginning the day in the 1950s that Bethlehem Steel began planning for its inevitable withdrawal, repercussions have been felt. For example, the company gradually removed itself from housing by selling off its entire stock in the late 1950s. The company devalued its property a half-million dollars a year, beginning in 1954, until the borough had difficulty maintaining municipal services. Sons of miners could no longer count on jobs in the mines or even near home. In short, all of life had to be reshaped around the absence of the supporting presence of the "company."

Presently, what is left are the memories of Camelot, memories which are based on the exploits of brave men, the achievements of future-oriented engineers, and the concern of the representatives of a paternalistic twentieth-century industrial giant. In short, these are memories based on a benign system of private work and enterprise. But even such a system of private enterprise, as we now know, could not possibly be sustained in the old setting of an earlier stage of industrialization. Outside forces intruded inevitably.